The No-Cook, No-Bake Cookbook

101 Delicious Recipes for When It's Too Hot to Cook

Matt Kadey

10/2013

Ulysses Press

Published by
Ulysses Press
P.O. Box 3440
Berkeley, CA 94703
www.ulyssespress.com

ISBN: 978-1-61243-189-5
Library of Congress Catalog Number 2013930885

Printed in Korea by Tara TPS through Four Colour Printing

10 9 8 7 6 5 4 3 2 1

Acquisitions Editor: Kelly Reed
Managing Editor: Claire Chun
Editor: Susan Lang
Proofreader: Lauren Harrison
Cover design and layout: what!design @ whatweb.com
Photographs: © Matt Kadey

3 3988 10113 7799

Table of Contents

Introduction

Let me begin by explaining how the concept for this cookbook came about. My girlfriend and I live in a generally wonderful house that predates the First World War. Unfortunately, the kitchen is situated on the second floor and we don't have air-conditioning. So the kitchen can get way too hot for comfort during the summer months. As a professional recipe developer for several magazines, I'm often employed by publications that work several months in advance and need seasonally appropriate dishes. The upshot is that during a sultry July heat wave, I could very well be roasting a batch of root vegetables or baking a pizza.

It's during these sweaty cooking sessions with the fan humming along that my appetite for cook-free meals and snacks increases proportionally with the growing heat. And with summers in so many locations seemingly getting hotter and hotter, I thought it was about time to provide a book filled with no-cook recipes that will help you keep your cool when the mercury hits triple digits.

That means, when the heat is on you can give your oven a welcome reprieve and instead force your grater, blender, and food processor to work overtime to outsmart the dog-day heat. Far from carrot sticks, lifeless salads, and PB&J sandwiches, creative no-cook meals, including appetizers and desserts, can provide a balance of convenience, nutrition, and gourmet taste — especially if you're willing to step outside of your normal culinary repertoire. No-cook recipes can also be the perfect solution to eating healthy even when you're in a time crunch.

By no means does no-cook cooking have to be relegated to the summer months. Cool dishes like Root Vegetable Salami Salad with Maple Vinaigrette (page 91) and Applesauce Pie (page 139) are well suited to the arrival of sweater weather. Also, you'll notice that the use of items like smoked fish, rotisserie chicken, and ricotta cheese ensures that this is not a raw cookbook. Don't get me wrong, I adore in-season raw kale and chewy soaked raw oats, but I also have a soft spot for quality prosciutto and tinned sardines.

Go ahead and master the art of chilling out by making these no-cook dishes the focal point of your summer or harried weeknight menu. I'll be jealous when it's scorching outside and I'm developing a Thanksgiving turkey recipe.

In Good Taste

Here's how to add a bonanza of flavor (and nutrition) to your no-cook meals and snacks.

Hug a farmer: Because you're most often serving veggies and fruits raw when shunning the oven, you'll want to make sure that the products you use are top-notch. Farmer's markets are the best place to load up on an array of fruits and vegetables that are at their nutrition and flavor peaks. Plus, it's a way to support your local economy, and many times the prices are lower than what you'll find at the supermarket.

Slice thinly: Finely slicing vegetables such as beets, carrots, and zucchini makes them much more delicate tasting to better tickle your palate.

Just add smoke: Infusing dishes with smoky ingredients like smoked paprika, smoked salmon, and chipotle chile pepper in abodo sauce can add a lot of interest. Also, consider keeping some smoked salt on hand to sprinkle on dishes like cold soups and crispy salads to make them pop.

Hooray for herbs: Summer is the perfect time to amplify salads, soups, and sauces with the sunniness of fresh herbs like basil and mint. Save the dried stuff for your winter stews.

Spice it up: I always make sure to have a wide assortment of spices in the kitchen to enliven no-cook dishes with their spicy, warming, or astringent personality. Many, such as cinnamon and cayenne, are gaining attention in research circles for their antioxidant might.

Taste of Asia: I find that classic Asian flavors like sesame oil, fish sauce, and sweet chili sauce work wonderfully in no-cook dishes. This perfect pairing is played out in many recipes in this book.

Go ahead and splurge: When you don't cook the heck out of foods it's harder to mask poor-quality ingredients. So it's worth paying a little extra for better quality when it comes to items such as canned seafood, canned beans, and nuts, as that will most certainly bring better flavors to the table. For example, compare the taste of mass-produced canned tuna or salmon with that from a smaller-scale business like Wild Planet. Once you do opt for better quality, it will be a challenge to go back.

Extra extracts: I keep a good selection of extracts such as vanilla, almond, and chocolate to punch up my no-cook breakfast and dessert recipes. Nielsen-Massey has a big selection of these marvelous flavor boosters.

Zest for life: The grated outermost portion of limes, lemons, oranges, and other citrus fruits can instantly add bright yet not overwhelming citrus flavor to a variety of no-cook savory and sweet dishes. When zesting, be careful to remove only the outermost layer of peel and not the white pith, which is unpleasantly bitter. Since you will be eating the fruit peel, make sure to give citrus a good wash before zesting and consider buying organic if you're concerned about pesticide residues that may concentrate in the rind.

Tools of the Trade

Outfit your kitchen with these tools to get the most out of no-cook cooking and to speed up the prep work.

Blender: Like chocolate, not all blenders are created equal. When it comes to this kitchen workhorse, you'll get what you pay for. I can't function in the kitchen without my trusty high-powered Vitamix, which I fire up several times a day for everything from smoothies to soups to homemade nut butters. If the steep price tag is hard too swallow, just make sure to get a blender with an ice-crushing function and a variable speed dial. A decent blender with some horsepower can be had for around a hundred bucks.

Chef's knife: Inevitably, no-cook cooking can entail lots of chopping, slicing, and mincing. To greatly ease your job and make it safer for your fingers, invest in a top-notch knife that is seriously sharp. Avoid those cheap knife sets from the big box stores and visit a culinary store with a good selection of fine knives from places like Germany and Japan. A chef's knife, paring knife, and bread knife will cover about 99 percent of your chopping needs. Good ones will last a lifetime, making them a worthwhile investment if there ever was one.

Citrus juicer or wooden reamer: These cone-shaped devices are handy for extracting the most juice possible from citrus like lemons and limes.

Electric kettle: Go electric for an efficient and quick way to boil water for dishes like no-cook soups and oatmeal, and without heating up the kitchen like a stovetop kettle would.

Food processor: This must-have machine is ideal for quickly chopping and mincing items like dried fruits, canned beans, and whole nuts or other situations where a blender doesn't work very well due to the lack of liquid. Many come with attachments for slicing and shredding, too.

Julienne vegetable peeler: Similar to a normal vegetable peeler but with a serrated blade, this handy tool makes creating long, thin strips of firm produce such as zucchini, carrot, and green mango a breeze. Oxo is a reliable brand.

Mandoline: The razor-sharp angled blade lets you make precise and uniform paper-thin slices of fruits and vegetables such as tomatoes, zucchini, beets, carrots, and apples. For safety reasons, avoid cheap, flimsy plastic models. Instead, opt for a sturdier plastic one or splurge on stainless steel. The mandoline that I use and trust is from Mastrad (www.mastrad.us).

Microplane: In a world of space-hogging kitchen gizmos, the diminutive Microplane zester/grater proves great things can come in small packages. Grab hold of the plastic handle and use the tiny blades to go to town on citrus zest, Parmesan cheese, dark chocolate, whole nutmeg, or even garlic and ginger.

Mortar and pestle: The grinding, crushing, and mashing action of this Stone Age food processor bursts the cell walls of items like fresh herbs and whole spices, releasing impressive amounts of fragrant flavor. To use, place foods in the mortar and push down with the pestle, using a twisting downward motion. With hard items like peppercorns and coffee beans, lightly pound first to form cracks. Choose a mortar and pestle made of a strong material such as granite that's not prone to chipping.

How to Use This Book

Accompanying many of the recipes in this book are these symbols:

- *V* vegetarian: The recipe is vegetarian, meaning it doesn't contain any meat or seafood. It may contain dairy.
- *G* gluten-free: The recipe is free of any gluten-containing products such as wheat flour.
- *L* leftover: When completely assembled, the recipe will maintain good texture and taste for two or more days. While the components of certain recipes such as Smoked Salmon Arugula Pesto Sandwiches (page 78) and Sunflower Tomato Pâté Nori Rolls (page 60) are indeed

perfectly fine for a number of days in the refrigerator, they don't
necessarily make good leftovers when everything is stacked or rolled
together.

Keeping in the spirit of no-cook cooking, none of the recipes on these
pages require the use of conventional cooking devices such as the oven,
stovetop, or microwave. However, in some situations I do use an electric
kettle or a toaster, neither of which will do much to steam up your kitchen
or do what I consider "cooking." A trusty electric kettle is a much more
energy-efficient method to boil water than a stovetop kettle and can open
the door to many creative no-cook possibilities.

A good number of the recipes in this book can be adjusted based on your
preference and the products you have on hand. Case in point: Trail Mix
Cups (page 16) will work wonderfully with any number of nut, seed, and
liquid sweetener combinations. If you have special dietary needs, I am
confident you can stay within the spirit of many of these recipes to make
them work for you. For example, if nut allergies are a concern, simply swap
out the peanuts for sunflower seeds in Asian-Style Celery Sticks (page 50).
If gluten tussles with your tummy, you can use oats labeled "gluten-free" or
quinoa flakes for Applesauce Pie (page 139).

As much as possible, I tried to base these recipes on whole foods not
weighed down by sketchy ingredients. When purchasing no-cook items
like breads and crackers, be diligent and scan the ingredients list for the
least confusing rundown possible. If many of the ingredients sound as if
they belong in a chemistry lab, take a pass.

I understand that many people will be put off by the use of canned foods
in a number of the recipes. But there is no reason to ixnay them for your
pantry. The quality of canned items like beans and seafood has improved
greatly in recent years thanks to forward-thinking companies like Eden
Foods and Wild Planet. The former provides a wide selection of canned
organic beans that are free of added salt, and the latter sells a range
of canned sustainably harvested seafood that truly tastes great. What's
more, an increasing number of companies like the aforementioned are
shunning the use of bisphenol-A (BPA), a chemical linked to coronary
and reproductive woes but one that lines the insides of many food
cans. So quality canned items can be just the ticket for busy cooks with
discriminating palates.

Breakfast and Brunch

Have hectic mornings caused your breakfast to morph into a cup of joe and a sugary muffin as you dash to the office? Well, if you're feeling too harried to stand frantically over a pot of simmering oatmeal, it's time to embrace the no-cook breakfast. From Breakfast Prosciutto Pear Sandwiches (page 23) to Overnight Oats (page 8) to tangy Avocado Fruit Salad (page 14), the recipes that follow are designed to be your friend when the clock is not, but you still want to jump-start your day with a good balance of carbohydrates, protein, and healthy fats. Or shift away from a comforting bowl of steamy oatmeal and start your summer morning with refreshing Pineapple Blueberry Smoothie (page 31) or one of the other smoothies in this chapter. Not only are frothy smoothies quick and portable, but they're packed with the necessary nutrients to get your day started right. And, as superfood recipes such as creamy Quinoa Hot Cereal with Cherry Sauce (page 24) show, a no-cook breakfast doesn't necessarily have to be served cold.

Overnight Oats

In our busy world, few people have time to cook up hearty steel-cut oats in the morning. Thankfully, soaking steel-cut oats overnight softens their texture so they can be enjoyed uncooked. The result is a deliciously chewy and filling breakfast cereal. Gelatinous chia seeds help soak up the liquid and their nutrient levels make many other foods jealous. Flaked coconut, dried fruit, diced apple, and sliced banana are among the many other topping possibilities. You can keep the prepared oats in the fridge for up to four days.   *Serves 4 or 5   V, L*

2 cups steel-cut oats

½ cup almond or hazelnut flour (optional)

3 tablespoons chia seeds

2 tablespoons pure maple syrup

1 teaspoon vanilla extract

1 teaspoon ground cinnamon

½ teaspoon ground nutmeg

2 cups milk of choice, plus more for serving

½ cup chopped nuts such as walnuts or almonds

1 cup berries of choice

Add the oats, almond or hazelnut flour, if using, chia seeds, maple syrup, vanilla, cinnamon, and nutmeg to a large container (preferably glass) and stir the contents together. Pour in the milk and stir again. Cover the container securely and refrigerate overnight.

Spoon the oat mixture into serving bowls and top with additional milk, nuts, berries, and more maple syrup if desired.

Top: OVERNIGHT OATS, *page 8*

Bottom: APRICOT RICOTTA BAGELS, *page 10*

Apricot Ricotta Bagels

Here's a wondrous breakfast to enjoy while sitting on the porch on a lazy weekend morning. It's equally good with other stone fruits like peaches, nectarines, or plums. Ricotta cheese is rich in protein, while pistachios provide a boost of beneficial fats. I'll often sprinkle the tops with additional cinnamon or add a light drizzle of honey.   *Serves 2   V*

1 cup low-fat ricotta cheese

1 tablespoon honey

½ teaspoon ground cinnamon

½ teaspoon vanilla extract

2 bagels of choice, sliced in half

4 fresh apricots, thinly sliced

¼ cup coarsely chopped pistachios

In a small bowl, stir together the ricotta cheese, honey, cinnamon, and vanilla. Toast the bagel halves. Spread the cheese mixture on the toasted bagels, and top with apricot slices and pistachios.

Creamy Banana Oatmeal with Coffee Plum Compote

You'll jump out of bed before the alarm for this comforting bowl of oatmeal bejeweled with a rich-tasting coffee-fruit sauce. You can substitute fresh plums for dried figs or dates, if you'd like. Extra sauce is also dazzling strewn over yogurt. If you want some crunch, swap out the almond butter for chopped almonds.   *Serves 2 or 3*   *V, G (if using 100% gluten-free oats)*

1 cup pitted dried plums (prunes)	*2 cups water*
1 cup brewed coffee	*3 tablespoons non-instant milk powder*
1 whole star anise	*1½ cups quick-cook oats*
1 teaspoon grated orange zest or orange extract	*1 large ripe banana, mashed*
1 teaspoon vanilla extract or coffee extract	*2 tablespoons unsalted almond butter or natural peanut butter*
	½ teaspoon ground cinnamon

Place the dried plums in a medium bowl and add the coffee, star anise, and orange zest or extract. Let soak overnight in the refrigerator.

Remove the star anise and discard. Add the plum mixture to a blender or food processor container along with the vanilla or coffee extract, and blend just until the plums are broken down. The mixture will be thick.

Bring water to a strong boil in an electric kettle. Add 2 cups boiled water to a large heatproof bowl along with the milk powder and whisk until most of the powder is dissolved. Stir in the oats, banana, almond or peanut butter, and cinnamon. Cover and let stand 5 minutes.

Spoon the oatmeal into serving bowls, and stir in the plum sauce.

Acai Granola Bowl

Açaí na tigela ("acai in the bowl") is a popular Brazilian treat made by blending antioxidant-rich acai fruit. My version whirls in pasteurized egg whites for a protein bump. If not using liquid egg whites, you'll need to add a little extra milk to produce a smooth consistency. You can also use a combination of frozen acai puree, such as that from the company Sambazon, and fresh bananas. In addition to granola, other garnish options include cacao nibs, coconut flakes, and fresh fruit such as berries.　　*Serves 2*　　*V*

2 frozen large bananas

½ cup milk of choice

½ cup pasteurized egg whites

3 tablespoons acai powder

1 tablespoon honey or pure maple syrup

½ cup granola of choice

Place the banana, milk, egg whites, acai, and honey or maple syrup in a food processor container or container of a high-powered blender such as a Vitamix, and blend until the consistency is thick and smooth. Add a few more splashes of milk if needed to help with blending. Scrape the mixture into serving bowls and top with granola.

Top: ACAI GRANOLA BOWL, *page 12*

Bottom: AVOCADO FRUIT SALAD, *page 14*

Avocado Fruit Salad

Here's a recipe to add some flair to brunch time. Nutritious avocado adds a creamy textural contrast to this fruit salad and helps cut some of the acidity. Pleasantly bitter cacao nibs add crunch, not to mention an antioxidant payload, so sprinkle them on top if you can get your hands on some. Other fruit possibilities include grapefruit, peaches, mango, strawberries, pineapple, and grapes. Also consider stirring some granola into the fruit mixture.   *Serves 4   V, G, L*

1 large orange

1 large banana, thinly sliced

2 kiwifruit, peeled and sliced

1 cup blackberries

1 ripe large avocado, cubed

¼ cup chopped walnuts

¼ cup coconut flakes

Zest of 1 lime

Juice of 1 lime, divided

1½ cups plain, low-fat yogurt

2 tablespoons honey

1 teaspoon vanilla extract or orange extract

¼ cup cacao nibs (optional)

Peel the orange, separate into segments, and slice each segment into thirds. Add to a large bowl and toss with the banana, kiwifruit, blackberries, avocado, walnuts, coconut flakes, lime zest, and half of the lime juice.

In a small bowl, whisk together the yogurt, remaining lime juice, honey, and vanilla or orange extract. Spoon the fruit mixture into serving bowls, and top with the yogurt mixture and cocoa nibs if using.

Cantaloupe Bowls

These edible bowls are a refreshing and nutritious way to kick-start your day. If desired, honeydew melon can replace the cantaloupe. If possible, seek out a granola that's lower in added sugar.　*Serves 2　V*

1 cup plain, low-fat Greek yogurt or low-fat cottage cheese

1 cup granola of choice

1 tablespoon honey

1 tablespoon lemon juice

½ teaspoon ground ginger

1 large cantaloupe

1 teaspoon grated lemon zest

½ cup fresh raspberries

¼ cup chopped unsalted pistachios or other nut of choice

2 tablespoons chopped fresh mint (optional)

In a medium bowl, stir together the yogurt or cottage cheese, granola, honey, lemon juice, and ginger.

Slice the cantaloupe in half along its width, and then slice about ½ inch off the bottoms so they sit flat. Scoop out the seeds and stuff the yogurt or cottage cheese mixture into each cavity. Top with lemon zest, raspberries, nuts, and mint if using.

Trail Mix Cups

These chewy morsels are packed with nutritional goodness courtesy of whole grain oats, nuts, and seeds. Enjoy two for breakfast or one for a mood-lifting snack during the day. They're also great for refilling your tank when tramping in the woods. Want 'em gluten-free? Use quinoa flakes or oats labeled "gluten-free."   *Serves 12   V, L*

1¼ cups rolled oats

¾ cup chopped pitted dates

½ cup unsalted raw or roasted almonds

½ cup unsalted raw or roasted cashews

½ cup dried cranberries or cherries

⅓ cup unsalted shelled raw or roasted
   sunflower seeds

2 tablespoons hemp seeds or chia seeds
   (optional)

2 tablespoons ground flaxseed

¼ teaspoon sea salt

½ cup finely chopped dark chocolate

⅓ cup honey

⅓ cup unsalted almond butter or
   unsalted natural peanut butter

Grated zest of 1 orange

1 teaspoon almond extract

Add the oats, dates, almonds, cashews, cranberries or cherries, sunflower seeds, hemp or chia seeds, flaxseed, and salt to a food processor container, and process until the oats and nuts are pulverized. Add the chocolate, honey, almond or peanut butter, orange zest, and almond extract, and process until the mixture clumps together.

Divide the mixture among 12 greased or paper-lined standard-size muffin cups, and press down firmly to pack in the contents. Place the tray in the freezer for about 30 minutes to harden up. Unmold the cups and store them in an airtight container in the refrigerator.

Top: TRAIL MIX CUPS, *page 16*

Bottom: SMOKED SALMON BREAKFAST CRACKERS, *page 18*

Smoked Salmon Breakfast Crackers

Smoked salmon is a much-enjoyed brunch item for many. Try it with this sweet and creamy avocado spread and you'll be a convert, too. Using rye crackers made mostly with whole rye flour ensures that your breakfast will be richer in hunger-fighting fiber.   *Serves 2 to 4*

1 medium ripe avocado	*Pinch of sea salt*
4 ounces cream cheese (about ⅔ cup)	*8 rye crackers or crispbreads*
1 tablespoon honey	*4 to 6 ounces smoked salmon*
1 teaspoon grated orange zest	*1 tablespoon chopped chives*

In a medium bowl, mash the avocado flesh with a fork. With a spoon, blend in the cream cheese, honey, orange zest, and salt.

Spread the avocado mixture on the crackers, and top with smoked salmon and chives.

Cheesy Fruit Wraps with Berry Coulis

Somewhat like cheesecake in a roll form, these wraps are a fun way to sneak more fruit into a child's breakfast or after-school snack. Or serve them as part of a weekend brunch. The sunflower seeds add some healthy crunch. There are many other fruit possibilities including kiwifruit, grapes, peaches, pears, and cherries. The wraps are best enjoyed slightly chilled, so try placing them in the freezer for a few minutes before serving. I'll often use a combination of strawberries and blackberries for the coulis, a fancy word for a sweet sauce commonly made with berries. *Serves 4   V, L*

Wraps:

4 ounces cream cheese (about ⅔ cup)

1 tablespoon honey

½ teaspoon vanilla extract

1 teaspoon grated orange zest (optional)

4 (8-inch) whole wheat tortillas

1 medium apple, cored and thinly sliced

1½ cups thinly sliced fresh strawberries

1 large ripe banana, thinly sliced

¼ cup unsalted raw or roasted shelled sunflower seeds

Coulis:

1 cup berries of choice, larger ones chopped

2 tablespoons honey, agave syrup, or granulated sugar

1 tablespoon lemon juice

2 tablespoons water

For the wraps: In a small bowl, stir together the cream cheese, honey, vanilla, and orange zest. Divide the cream cheese mixture among the tortillas, spreading it all the way to the edges. Arrange apple and strawberry slices in a single layer on the tortillas. Top with banana slices and sunflower seeds.

Tightly roll up each tortilla toward the top, pushing in any fruit that wiggles out. Gently press down and slice each roll in half.

For the coulis: Combine the berries, sweetener, and lemon juice in a food processor or blender container and let sit 5 minutes. Add the water to the mixture, and puree until completely smooth. Strain through a fine-mesh sieve, stirring and pressing with a wooden spoon or spatula to remove seeds and any skins.

Serve the wraps with the berry sauce on the side for dipping.

Spelt Muesli

In Europe (most notably Switzerland), muesli is a cherished uncooked breakfast cereal made from toasted rolled oats, nuts, and dried fruits. This hearty version makes use of spelt, an ancient cousin of wheat thought to be more nutrient dense than today's hybridized wheat varieties. Quinoa flakes, rye flakes, rice puffs, and toasted rolled oats are good substitutes, however. If they're available, definitely try dried goldenberries, which absolutely burst with sweet and sour flavor in your mouth. But chopped dried apricots will work, too. In the winter, try serving the muesli with warmed milk. You can also use this recipe layered with yogurt and fruit in a breakfast parfait.   *Serves 6   V, L*

1½ cups spelt flakes

1 cup chopped pecans or other nuts

½ cup flaked coconut

½ cup raisins, dried currants, or dried blueberries

½ cup dried goldenberries or chopped dried apricots

⅓ cup shelled unsalted raw or roasted sunflower seeds

⅓ cup ground flaxseed or toasted wheat germ

¼ cup hemp seeds (optional)

1 teaspoon ground allspice

Pinch of sea salt

Milk or yogurt, for serving

Fruit of choice, for serving

In a large storage container, stir together all the ingredients. To serve, place the muesli in a serving bowl and top with a desired amount of milk of choice or yogurt as well as any amount of fresh fruit such as blueberries, chopped apples, or sliced banana. Letting the flakes soak for a few moments will soften them.

Top: SPELT MUESLI, *page 20*
Bottom: WAFFLES WITH ALMOND CREAM AND PEACH SAUCE, *page 22*

Waffles with Almond Cream and Peach Sauce

Thankfully for those of us without a waffle maker, store-bought frozen waffles have gotten a lot more nutritious and better tasting in recent years. Still, make sure the first ingredient listed is a whole grain such as whole wheat flour. Then use this dynamic almond, peach, and cheese trio to gussy them up. Greek yogurt is a topping option, as well.   *Serves 4   V*

2 ripe peaches, chopped

1 teaspoon minced fresh ginger

1 teaspoon grated lemon zest or lemon
   extract

½ teaspoon ground cinnamon

⅓ cup unsalted almond butter

3 tablespoons low-fat evaporated milk

2 tablespoons pure maple syrup

1 teaspoon vanilla extract

8 frozen whole grain waffles

1 cup low-fat ricotta cheese or low-fat
   cottage cheese

Place the peaches, ginger, lemon zest or extract, and cinnamon in a blender or food processor container, and blend until combined but still chunky.

To make the almond cream, combine the almond butter, evaporated milk, maple syrup, and vanilla in a blender or food processor container. Blend until the mixture is creamy. Add additional evaporated milk if needed to reach the desired consistency.

Prepare the waffles according to package directions. Top with almond cream, peach sauce, and a dollop or two of ricotta or cottage cheese.

Breakfast Prosciutto Pear Sandwiches

This salty-sweet combo is sure to stoke your taste buds and enliven breakfast or brunch time. Or include a slice of cheese such as provolone or sharp cheddar and call it lunch. For the fig jam, you can also use orange juice or dark grape juice in lieu of apple cider with good results, and sliced apples are a possible substitution for the pears.   *Serves 4*

1 cup halved dried Mission figs, stems sliced off

½ cup apple cider

¼ teaspoon ground cloves

4 English muffins, preferably whole grain, split in half

4 tablespoons almond butter

8 slices prosciutto (about 2 ounces)

2 medium pears, thinly sliced

Place the figs in a bowl, cover with cold water, and soak for about 2 hours. Drain the figs and place them in a food processor or blender container along with the apple cider and cloves. Blend until just a little chunky.

Toast the English muffins halves until crisp. Spread almond butter and fig jam on four of the muffin halves. Top with prosciutto and pear slices. Place the remaining muffin halves on top and slice in half.

Quinoa Hot Cereal with Cherry Sauce

Quinoa flakes are made by passing whole quinoa seeds through a roller to flatten them. The quick-cooking flakes make for a nutritious breakfast cereal when teamed with spices, nuts, and dried fruit. Look for them in health food stores or well-stocked bulk shops. Incorporating milk powder produces a richer consistency and provides a morning dose of calcium. For convenience, I'll often use frozen and thawed pitted cherries for the topping.   *Serves 2   V, G*

2 cups water	1 teaspoon ground cinnamon
3 tablespoons non-instant milk powder	¼ teaspoon ground nutmeg
1 cup quinoa flakes	1 cup pitted fresh or frozen and thawed cherries
½ cup chopped pitted dates, pitted dried plums (prunes), or dried figs	2 tablespoons pure maple syrup
⅓ cup chopped walnuts	½ teaspoon almond extract

Bring water to a boil in an electric kettle. Add 2 cups boiled water along with the milk powder to a large bowl and whisk until dissolved. Stir in the quinoa flakes, dried fruit, walnuts, cinnamon, and nutmeg. Let sit covered for 2 minutes.

Meanwhile, place the cherries, maple syrup, and almond extract in a blender or food processor container, and blend until the cherries are broken down but still slightly chunky. Avoid overprocessing the mixture into juice.

Spoon the quinoa cereal into serving bowls and top with cherry sauce.

Top: QUINOA HOT CEREAL WITH CHERRY SAUCE, *page 24*

Bottom: PEANUT BUTTER PUMPKIN BARS, *page 26*

Peanut Butter Pumpkin Bars

A medley of carefully matched ingredients ensures that each bite of these moist no-bake bars is more intriguing than the last. The molasses adds richness, but a dark grade of maple syrup will work, too. For a little extra protein, you can replace the milk powder with protein powder.

Serves 6 to 12   V, L

¾ cup unsalted natural peanut butter or other nut butter of choice

¾ cup canned pumpkin puree

2 tablespoons molasses

2 cups granola of choice, plus more for topping

½ cup oat bran

½ cup non-instant milk powder

⅓ cup dried currants

½ teaspoon ground cinnamon

½ teaspoon ground ginger

¼ teaspoon ground cloves

Pinch of sea salt

Place the peanut butter, pumpkin, and molasses in a large bowl and mix until well combined. Add all the remaining ingredients and mix until everything is moist. The mixture should be thick.

Place the mixture in a greased or parchment paper–lined 8-inch-square baking pan, and spread it out until you have an even thickness of about ½ inch. Sprinkle some additional granola on top and press down lightly. Place the pan in the freezer until firm, about 1 hour. Slice into 12 bars and store in an airtight container in the refrigerator.

Spread the Love

Making your own spreads for morning toast is much easier than you may think. And the results are truly flavorsome. Here are a handful of praiseworthy options.

Blueberry Chia Jam

3 tablespoons chia seeds

1¼ cups water

1½ cups blueberries

3 tablespoons sugar of choice

½ teaspoon ground cinnamon or allspice

In a bowl, mix together the chia seeds and water. Let sit for at least 30 minutes to form a gel, stirring with a whisk occasionally to prevent clumping. Place the chia seed gel in a blender or food processor container along with the remaining ingredients. Pulse a few times until just combined. Place the jam in the refrigerator overnight before serving. Store in the refrigerator for up to a week.

Chocolate Cashew Butter

2 cups unsalted roasted whole cashews

¼ cup unsweetened cocoa powder

3 tablespoons honey

2 tablespoons oil of choice

Place all the ingredients in a food processor or high-powered blender such as a Vitamix and blend on high until the mixture becomes creamy, 2 to 5 minutes, depending on the machine you're using. The cashews will go through stages: first chopped, then lumpy, and finally smooth as they release their oils. If using a Vitamix, make sure to use the tamper to press the ingredients into the blades. If using a food processor, you will likely need to wipe down the sides a couple of times during blending. If the mixture isn't becoming smooth enough, you can add a little extra oil to help smooth it out. Store in the refrigerator for about 1 month.

Apricot Orange Marmalade

1 cup dried apricots

2 teaspoons grated orange zest

Juice of 1 medium orange

½ teaspoon ground allspice

½ teaspoon ground ginger

½ teaspoon almond extract (optional)

Place the apricots, orange zest, orange juice, allspice, and ginger in a wide-mouth jar. Add enough cold water to cover the contents by just ½ inch. Cover and soak for at least 8 hours. Place the apricot mixture, remaining liquid, and almond extract if using in a blender or food processor container. Pulse until mixture turns into a chunky paste. Store in the refrigerator for up to 2 weeks.

Almond Pecan Flax Butter

1 cup unsalted raw or roasted almonds

1 cup pecan halves

¼ cup ground flaxseed

1 tablespoon oil of choice

Place all the ingredients in a food processor or high-powered blender such as a Vitamix and blend on high until the mixture becomes creamy, 2 to 5 minutes, depending on the machine you're using. The nuts will go through stages: first chopped, then lumpy, and finally smooth. If using a Vitamix, make sure to use the tamper to press the ingredients into the blades. If using a food processor, you will likely need to wipe down the sides a couple of times during blending. If the mixture isn't becoming creamy enough, you can add a little extra oil to help smooth it out. Store in the refrigerator for about 1 month.

Cinnamon Maple Raisin Butter

1 stick (½ cup) unsalted butter, softened

⅓ cup raisins

3 tablespoons pure maple syrup

1 teaspoon vanilla extract

½ teaspoon ground cinnamon

Pinch of salt

Place all the ingredients in a food processor container and blend until the mixture clumps together. You can also vigorously whip the mixture together by hand in a large bowl. Refrigerate for up to 2 weeks or you can roll the butter into a log in plastic wrap and freeze until needed.

Carrot Orange Smoothie Cups

For speed and convenience, these icy smoothie cups are perfect for chaotic mornings, an afternoon pick-me-up, or a healthy after-school snack for the tykes. When you're ready for a creamy smoothie, just drop a couple of the frozen cups into a blender with some additional liquid and you're good to go. Carrot juice has an earthy, sweet flavor that's great in smoothies, but feel free to play with other flavor combinations using this method. For the easiest extraction of the smoothie cups, I use bendable silicone muffin cups.   *Serves 6   V, G, L*

1½ cups carrot juice

2 large oranges, peeled and quartered

1 cup plain, low-fat yogurt

Juice of ½ lemon

2 tablespoons tahini (sesame paste)

2 tablespoons honey

2 teaspoons chopped fresh ginger

1 teaspoon ground allspice

1½ cups water or coconut water

Place all the ingredients except for the water or coconut water in a blender container and blend until smooth.

Divide the mixture among 12 medium standard-size muffin cups, place the tray in the freezer, and freeze until solid, about 4 hours.

Unmold the smoothie cups, place them in an airtight container, and return them to the freezer until ready to use. If you did not use silicone muffin cups or liners and are having trouble unmolding the frozen cups, try placing the bottom of the muffin tin in warm water for a few seconds, being careful not to thaw the contents.

When ready to make a smoothie, place the water or coconut water and two smoothie cups in a blender container and blend until smooth. For most blenders, it's best to slice the smoothie cups into halves or quarters first before placing them in the blender container. If you want a more substantial smoothie, blend in extras like additional yogurt, pasteurized egg whites, milk powder, or protein powder.

Matcha Mango Shake

Matcha is derived from the words *mo cha*, "to grind tea" in Chinese parlance, and by grinding the tea leaves into a fine powder, you ingest the whole tea leaves instead of only the water steeped in them. The upshot is that you take in a huge dose of disease-thwarting antioxidants. For me, no day is complete without a warm cup of matcha tea, but the verdant powder is equally wonderful in smoothies. Find it at well-stocked tea stores or online at www.matchasource.com. I often make this shake using coconut milk from cartons, which is less rich than canned coconut milk. Undetectable silken tofu adds a shot of protein.   *Serves 2   V, G*

2 cups milk of choice

½ block (about ½ cup) soft tofu

2 tablespoons flaked coconut

1 tablespoon honey

1 teaspoon matcha powder

¼ teaspoon ground ginger

1 cup frozen mango cubes

Place all the ingredients into a blender container and blend until smooth, about 30 seconds. If desired, serve with a dusting of matcha on top.

Pineapple Blueberry Smoothie

It's blue, but there is nothing sad about this smoothie. Liquid ambrosia, indeed! Pasteurized carton egg whites such as AllWhites are found in the egg section of the grocery store and are perfectly safe to use in smoothies. Along with whole grain quinoa flakes, tangy coconut water, and healthy fat from almonds, the protein in the egg whites makes this drink a complete nutritional package. You can replace the quinoa flakes with spelt flakes or quick-cook oats if desired. If using fresh blueberries, add about four ice cubes for a colder smoothie.   *Serves 2   G*

2 cups coconut water

1 cup pineapple chunks

⅓ cup quinoa flakes

½ cup pasteurized egg whites

¼ cup unsalted raw or roasted almonds

1 teaspoon vanilla extract or ½ teaspoon almond extract

¼ teaspoon ground cloves

1 cup frozen blueberries

Place all the ingredients in a blender container and blend until smooth, about 30 seconds.

Java Cocoa Smoothie

Here's a way to get your morning nutrition and coffee fix all at once. Wheat germ offers a payload of vital nutrients, while a whisper of cardamom provides some mystery. To freeze a banana, peel it, slice into thirds, and store in a zip-top bag or airtight container in the freezer. On a blistery winter morning when you may not want a chilly smoothie, you can simply blend in warm coffee and a fresh banana.   *Serves 2   V*

2 cups brewed coffee, cooled to room temperature

½ cup low-fat ricotta cheese

3 tablespoons wheat germ

2 tablespoons unsalted almond butter or natural peanut butter

2 tablespoons unsweetened cocoa powder

¼ teaspoon ground cardamom

1 teaspoon vanilla extract, coffee extract, or chocolate extract

1 banana, preferably frozen

Place all the ingredients in a blender container and blend until smooth, about 30 seconds.

Starters and Sides

From refreshing soups to lively salads to a new twist on trail mix, here's a collection of light recipes that are certainly cool, so to speak. Try rolling up the Sunflower Tomato Pâté Nori Rolls (page 60) when your afternoon energy gauge is running near empty or whip up a perfectly sweet Peach Gazpacho (page 36) to avoid meltdown at mealtime. When it comes to stuffing beach-bound baskets or car-trip coolers, go for the easy breezy Watermelon Jicama Salad (page 39) or Mango Spring Rolls with Dipping Sauce (page 56). This chapter is also laced with appealing hors d'oeuvres ideas such as nut-crusted Cheese Date Balls (page 66) and Zucchini Smoked Fish Rolls (page 58) for when it's time to entertain a hungry crowd. Source local and seasonal ingredients for these recipes when possible, and you'll also help your body stockpile an enormous amount of vitamins and minerals for good health.

Chipotle Corn Soup with Cilantro Oil

When corn is at its seasonal peak, you certainly don't need to cook it to reap its flavor rewards. For this recipe, seek out sweeter varieties of the cobs. Blending navy beans and buttermilk into the soup makes it heartier, while an infusion of chipotle chile pepper gives it a smoky kick. Look for cans of chipotle peppers in adobo sauce in the Latin section of grocers. They pack a punch, so if you want your soup to be a little tamer, cut back on the amount used or simply omit it. As a substitute for chipotle, you can also use cayenne powder if desired.   *Serves 6   V, G, L*

3 ears of corn

2 cups low-sodium vegetable broth

1 cup buttermilk

1 cup canned white navy beans, rinsed and drained

2 cloves garlic, chopped

1 shallot, chopped

1 tablespoon fresh dill or thyme

2 teaspoons minced chipotle chile pepper in adobo sauce

½ teaspoon sea salt, divided

¼ teaspoon freshly ground black pepper

1 cup packed cilantro

⅓ cup extra virgin olive oil

1½ ounces (about ⅓ cup) diced feta cheese

To slice off the corn kernels, simply upend the cob in a bowl and use a sharp chef's knife to slice downward. When all the kernels are off, use the back of the knife to scrape off any additional corn juice.

Place the corn kernels, vegetable broth, buttermilk, beans, garlic, shallot, dill or thyme, chile pepper, ¼ teaspoon salt, and black pepper in a food processor or blender container, and blend until smooth. Refrigerate the soup for at least 2 hours.

To make the cilantro oil, add the cilantro, olive oil, and remaining ¼ teaspoon salt to a food processor or blender container and blend until smooth. Add a little more olive oil if necessary to help with blending. Pour the cilantro oil into a fine-mesh sieve set over a bowl and let drain 15 minutes (do not press on solids). Discard solids.

Ladle the soup into serving bowls and garnish with cilantro oil and feta cheese.

Carrot Soup

At once, this soup is sweet, spicy, and earthy. For a smoother texture, be sure to let your blender or food processor run for at least 1 minute to break down the fibers in the carrot. You can garnish with a dollop of sour cream if you wish.   *Serves 4   V, G, L*

2 cups apple juice

½ cup water

1 pound carrots (about 6 to 7 medium), peeled and chopped

1 cup plain, low-fat yogurt

2 tablespoons pure maple syrup

2 teaspoons chopped fresh ginger

1 teaspoon ground allspice

¼ teaspoon sea salt

⅛ teaspoon cayenne

¼ cup sliced pecans, for garnish

Place all the ingredients except the pecans in a blender or food processor container, and blend until very smooth, about 1 minute. Refrigerate for at least 2 hours before serving.

To serve, ladle the soup into serving bowls and garnish with pecans.

Peach Gazpacho

This riff on gazpacho is a cool refresher on a sultry day, and you might liken it to the taste of sunshine. When local peaches go out of season, consider using frozen as fresh imported peaches often are of poor quality. You can also garnish the soup with diced avocado.   *Serves 6*   *V, G, L*

⅔ cup water

2 pounds ripe peaches (about 6 medium), pitted and chopped

½ English cucumber, chopped

2 green onions (scallions), white and green parts, sliced

1 jalapeño chile pepper, seeded and minced (optional)

2 cloves garlic, minced

3 tablespoons chopped fresh basil

3 tablespoons extra virgin olive oil

2 tablespoons red wine vinegar

¼ teaspoon sea salt

¼ teaspoon freshly ground black pepper

1 small red bell pepper, diced, for garnish

1 small peach, diced, for garnish

Add the water, peaches, cucumber, green onion, jalapeño if using, garlic, basil, olive oil, vinegar, salt, and pepper to a blender or food processor container. Blend together until smooth. If you're using a small food processor or blender you may need to do this in batches. Refrigerate for at least 2 hours before serving.

When ready to serve, ladle the soup into serving bowls and garnish with bell pepper and peach.

Avocado Coconut Soup

Avocado lends this soup a creamy texture, while coconut milk gives it some tropical flavor. The handful of basil provides punch. For a lighter-tasting soup, I prefer to use shelf-stable coconut milk from a carton as opposed to canned coconut milk. When serving cold soups, try chilling the serving bowls, as well.   *Serves 4   V, G*

1½ cups coconut milk

1½ cups water

2 ripe large avocados

¼ cup packed fresh basil

Juice of 1 lime

1 jalapeño chile pepper, seeded and minced

¼ teaspoon sea salt

¼ teaspoon freshly ground pepper, preferably white

Grated zest of 1 lime

Place all the ingredients except the lime zest in a blender or food processor container, and blend until smooth. If you find the mixture too thick, simply blend in more coconut milk or water. Pour the mixture into a container with a tight-fitting lid and refrigerate for at least 2 hours.

When ready to serve, ladle the soup into serving bowls and garnish with lime zest.

Watermelon Jicama Salad

Providing a salty-sweet cool crunch, this salad featuring watermelon, summer's quintessential fruit, is tantamount to summer on a plate. Native to Mexico, jicama (pronounced HEE-kah-ma) has a crisp white flesh that tastes like a fusion of cucumber, pear, and water chestnut. If jicama is unavailable, replace it with cucumber.   *Serves 4   V, G, L*

5 cups seedless watermelon, sliced into 1-inch cubes

2 cups thinly sliced jicama

1 medium avocado, cubed

1 cup cubed feta cheese (about 3 ounces)

½ cup unsalted raw or roasted whole cashews

¼ cup chopped fresh basil

2 tablespoons chopped fresh mint

2 tablespoons extra virgin olive oil

Juice of ½ lemon

½ teaspoon sea salt

½ teaspoon freshly ground black pepper

¼ teaspoon red pepper flakes

In a large bowl, gently toss together the watermelon, jicama, avocado, feta cheese, cashews, basil, and mint.

In a small bowl, whisk together the olive oil, lemon juice, salt, pepper, and pepper flakes. Toss the watermelon and jicama mixture with the dressing. If time permits, chill for about 1 hour before serving.

Marinated Mushroom Salad

Low-calorie mushrooms have been shown to harbor a number of health-boosting compounds, so it's always a good idea to eat a lot of them. The marinade causes the edible fungi to release water and soften, resulting in a "cooked" toothsome texture. For a boost of protein, you could toss some salami or prosciutto in with the marinated mushrooms.   *Serves 4   V, G*

4 cups thinly sliced cremini mushrooms

1½ cups cherry tomatoes, sliced in half

¼ cup extra virgin olive oil

3 tablespoons white wine or 2 tablespoons white wine vinegar

1 clove garlic, minced

2 teaspoons Dijon mustard

2 teaspoons fresh thyme

1 teaspoon fennel seeds (optional)

½ teaspoon sea salt

¼ teaspoon freshly ground black pepper

⅓ cup coarsely chopped flat-leaf parsley

2 cups spinach or other greens of choice

⅓ cup chopped walnuts, for garnish

¼ cup grated Parmesan or Gruyère cheese, for garnish

Truffle oil, for garnish (optional)

In a large bowl or container, combine the mushrooms and tomatoes. In a small bowl, whisk together the oil, wine or vinegar, garlic, mustard, thyme, fennel seeds if using, salt, and black pepper. Add the oil mixture to the mushrooms and tomatoes, and toss to coat. Cover and let marinate in the refrigerator for at least 2 hours or up to overnight, stirring a couple of times.

Mix the parsley into the mushroom mixture. Arrange the spinach on serving plates and top with mushroom salad. Garnish with walnuts, grated cheese, and truffle oil if desired.

Lemony Apple Fennel Salad

With its slight licorice flavor and crunchy texture, fennel is wonderful served raw in salads. Grated carrot, sliced pear, canned tuna, goat cheese, slivered almonds, and parsley would be other stellar additions.

Serves 4   V, G

Salad:

- 1 fennel bulb, thinly sliced, fronds reserved for garnish
- 2 medium apples, thinly sliced
- 2 cups packed arugula
- 1 medium zucchini, shredded (about 1 cup)
- ¼ cup chopped fresh mint (optional)

Dressing:

- 3 tablespoons extra virgin olive oil
- 1 tablespoon honey
- Juice of ½ lemon
- 1 teaspoon grated lemon zest
- 1 clove garlic, minced
- ¼ teaspoon sea salt
- ¼ teaspoon freshly ground black pepper

For the salad: In a large bowl, toss together the fennel, apple, arugula, zucchini, and mint if using.

For the dressing: In a small bowl, whisk together the olive oil, honey, lemon juice, lemon zest, garlic, salt, and pepper.

Toss the salad with the dressing and serve garnished with fennel fronds.

Asparagus Ribbon Salad with Sesame Orange Dressing

Who says you have to cook asparagus? Shaved thinly, this harbinger of summer is delightfully earthy and tender after just a quick soak in hot water. For ease of peeling, make sure to use fatter spears as opposed to pencil-thin ones. You can prepare the salad up to one day in advance, but toss with the dressing just before serving. You can also toss in some baby spinach, watercress, or arugula.   *Serves 4   V, G*

Juice of ½ orange

1 clove garlic, minced

1 teaspoon finely minced fresh ginger

¼ teaspoon sea salt

¼ teaspoon freshly ground black pepper

2 teaspoons sesame oil

1 tablespoon grapeseed or other neutral-tasting oil

1 pound asparagus (about 1 bunch)

1 tablespoon sesame seeds, for garnish

In a small bowl, whisk together the orange juice, garlic, ginger, salt, and pepper. Whisk in the sesame oil and grapeseed oil. Set aside.

Trim the woody lower ends of the asparagus spears. Cut off the top tips from each stalk and slice the tips in half vertically; set aside. Working from the bottom up, run a vegetable peeler several times along the length of each stalk to make ribbons. Place the sliced tips and ribbons in a heatproof bowl. Bring 4 cups water to a boil using an electric kettle, pour over the asparagus, and let sit 1 minute. Drain and rinse under cold water. Pat dry with a paper towel or clean kitchen towel to remove as much water as possible.

Place the asparagus in a large bowl and toss with the orange dressing. Divide among serving plates and garnish with sesame seeds.

Top: ASPARAGUS RIBBON SALAD WITH SESAME ORANGE DRESSING, *page 42*

Bottom: SUMMER BERRY SALAD WITH POPPY SEED DRESSING, *page 44*

Summer Berry Salad with Poppy Seed Dressing

To some chefs, granola is the new crouton, lending salads pleasant crunch, and sun-kissed berries turn an already healthful salad of greens, herbs, and nuts into a nutritional standout. If not using feta, add a couple pinches of salt to the salad dressing. As with most salads, add the dressing just before serving to avoid soggy greens.　　*Serves 4 to 6*　　*V*

Salad:

6 cups salad greens

¼ cup coarsely chopped fresh mint

1 cup blueberries or blackberries

2 cups sliced strawberries

½ cup granola of choice

⅓ cup chopped unsalted almonds, walnuts, or other nut of choice

½ English cucumber, thinly sliced

3 ounces (about ½ cup) chopped feta cheese (optional)

Dressing:

Juice of ½ orange

1½ tablespoons balsamic vinegar

1 tablespoon honey

1 teaspoon poppy seeds

¼ teaspoon freshly ground black pepper

¼ cup extra virgin olive oil

For the salad: In a large bowl, toss together the salad greens, mint, blueberries or blackberries, strawberries, granola, nuts, cucumber, and feta cheese if using.

For the dressing: In a small bowl, stir together the orange juice, balsamic vinegar, honey, poppy seeds, and black pepper. Whisk in the olive oil.

Divide the salad among serving plates and top with poppy seed dressing.

Cucumber Seaweed Salad

Popular in Japanese cuisine, this light salad packs a ton of umami, courtesy of the seaweed. Soaking up nutrients as it dances in the currents, wakami and other edible seaweed are nutrition powerhouses and something we should be eating more of. If available, wasabi powder adds a little kick to the dressing. If you want to slightly pickle the cucumber, dress the salad about 10 minutes before serving.   *Serves 4   V, G*

1 ounce dried wakame seaweed strips

1 English cucumber

¼ teaspoon sea salt

4 red radishes, thinly sliced

2 green onions (scallions), white and green parts, thinly sliced

2 tablespoons rice vinegar

1 tablespoon reduced-sodium soy sauce

2 teaspoons sesame oil

2 teaspoons sugar of choice

1 teaspoon grated fresh ginger

1 teaspoon wasabi powder (optional)

1 tablespoon sesame seeds, preferably black, for garnish

Rehydrate the wakame according to the package directions. Squeeze out the excess water and chop into about 2-inch pieces.

Cut the cucumber in half lengthwise. Scoop out the seeds with a small spoon and slice thinly along the width. Sprinkle the salt over the cucumber slices, let stand for 5 minutes until soft and watery, then squeeze out excess water between a few sheets of paper towel or a clean kitchen towel.

In a large bowl, toss together the seaweed, cucumber, radish, and green onion. In a small bowl, whisk together the rice vinegar, soy sauce, sesame oil, sugar, ginger, and wasabi powder if using.

Divide the salad among serving plates and drizzle the dressing over top. Garnish with sesame seeds.

Goat Cheese Endive Boats

Adorable pale and crisp Belgian endive leaves provide an elegant counterpoint to tangy goat cheese topping. The filling can be prepared up to three days in advance. Store the endive heads wrapped in a damp paper towel inside a plastic bag in the refrigerator for up to five days.
Serves 8   V, G

4 ounces soft goat cheese (about 1 cup)

1 small apple, finely diced

1 tablespoon fresh thyme or chopped tarragon

1 shallot, finely chopped

Juice of ½ lemon

¼ teaspoon sea salt

¼ teaspoon freshly ground black pepper

16 Belgian endive leaves (about 2 endive heads), bottom core sliced off

¼ cup finely chopped walnuts

In a bowl, stir together the goat cheese, apple, tarragon or thyme, shallot, lemon juice, salt, and black pepper.

Arrange the endive leaves on a serving platter, and spoon a generous dollop of the goat cheese mixture on the paler end of each leaf. For visual appeal, leave the yellowish tops uncovered. Sprinkle walnuts over the filling.

Tomato Cherry Bruschetta

Cherries add a new twist and tempered sweetness to this classic appetizer, which works equally well as a side dish. Assemble just before serving to avoid soggy bread. Instead of using olive oil, you can try spreading some jarred roasted garlic spread on the bread slices. *Serves 6   V*

- *1 cup quartered cherry tomatoes*
- *1 cup fresh or frozen and thawed, pitted, and quartered cherries*
- *2 cloves garlic, finely minced*
- *1 green onion (scallion), white and green parts, thinly sliced*
- *2 tablespoons chopped fresh oregano or basil*
- *2 tablespoons extra virgin olive oil, plus more for bread*
- *1 tablespoon balsamic vinegar or red wine vinegar*
- *¼ teaspoon sea salt*
- *¼ teaspoon freshly ground black pepper*
- *1 loaf crusty bread, preferably whole grain*

In a large bowl, toss together the tomatoes, cherries, garlic, green onion, oregano or basil, olive oil, vinegar, salt, and pepper.

Cut the bread diagonally into slices about ½ inch thick. Toast the slices until golden and crisp. Drizzle a small amount of olive oil onto the bread slices, and spoon the tomato-cherry mixture on top.

Curry Deviled Eggs

This curry-infused version of a party classic is sure to disappear from the platter as fast as you can fill it. Available at most supermarkets, jarred picked eggs offer a way to enjoy the orbs minus the need for hard boiling or peeling. Creamy Greek-style yogurt is a good stand-in for sour cream, and to fancy things up try garnishing with picked jalapeño chile peppers or picked ginger. Sometimes, I even stir finely chopped sun-dried tomatoes into the yolk mixture. *Serves 6* *G, L*

6 jarred pickled eggs

⅓ cup low-fat sour cream

1 green onion (scallion), green part only, thinly sliced or 1 tablespoon chopped chives

1 teaspoon creamy Dijon mustard or regular yellow mustard

1 teaspoon curry powder

½ teaspoon paprika, preferably smoked, plus more for garnish

¼ teaspoon freshly ground black pepper

Slice each egg in half. Scoop out the yolks and place them in a medium bowl. Using the back of a fork, mash the yolks. Stir in the remaining ingredients until smooth.

Simply spoon the yolk mixture into the egg cavities or use a piping bag. If you don't have a piping bag, try a plastic sandwich bag. Place the yolks in the bag, squeeze all the filling down to one corner, snip off the corner tip, and squeeze from the top of the filling to pipe into the egg whites. Sprinkle with paprika and refrigerate until ready to serve.

Top: CURRY DEVILED EGGS, *page 48*

Bottom: ASIAN-STYLE CELERY STICKS, *page 50*

Asian-Style Celery Sticks

Here's how to make lowbrow celery sticks a little more fanciful.
Reminiscent of satay, the crunchy-sweet-salty bites will be a hit at parties
and potlucks or enjoyable as a midday snack. They are great as a healthy
after-school nibble for the kids, as well. Slicing a sliver off the bottom of
each celery stick creates a flat surface so they won't wobble when plated.
You can use almonds or even sunflower seeds if peanut allergies are a
concern. The spread will keep for about five days stored in an airtight
container in the refrigerator.   *Serves 6   V, G, L*

1 cup unsalted roasted peanuts

¼ cup coconut milk

2 tablespoons rice vinegar

1½ tablespoons sweet chili sauce, such
as Thai Kitchen

1 tablespoon reduced-sodium soy sauce
or tamari

2 teaspoons minced fresh ginger

2 teaspoons sesame oil

8 to 10 celery stalks, sliced into thirds

¼ cup finely diced dried pineapple or
mango (optional)

Place the peanuts in a food processor container and pulse until chopped
into small pieces. Add the coconut milk, rice vinegar, chili sauce, soy sauce,
ginger, and sesame oil. Blend until a slightly chunky paste forms, or until
desired consistency.

Spread the peanut mixture into the rib of each piece of celery.
Garnish with dried pineapple or mango if desired.

Beet Apple Slaw with Carrot Vinaigrette

When grated, raw beets are wonderfully sweet and very edible. The vibrant carrot dressing adds to the fetching presentation and provides a touch of added sweetness. You can use any extra carrot juice in your summer smoothies, such as Carrot Orange Smoothie Cups (page 29).

Serves 6   V, G, L

Slaw:

1 pound beets (about 3 medium), peeled

2 medium apples, peeled

2 green onions (scallions), white and green parts, thinly sliced

2 tablespoons chopped fresh mint or tarragon

Dressing:

⅓ cup carrot juice

2 tablespoons cider vinegar or rice vinegar

2 teaspoons honey

1 clove garlic, finely minced

1 tablespoon prepared horseradish

¼ teaspoon sea salt

¼ teaspoon freshly ground black pepper

⅓ cup extra virgin olive oil or walnut oil

For the Slaw: Grate the beets and apples into a large bowl using a box grater or mandoline. If the apples are very juicy, it's best to press out some of the water between sheets of paper towel or a clean kitchen towel. Toss the grated beets and apples with the green onion and mint or tarragon.

For the Dressing: In a separate bowl, whisk together the carrot juice, vinegar, honey, garlic, horseradish, salt, and pepper. Whisk in the oil.

Place the slaw on serving plates and drizzle carrot dressing over the top.

Kale Slaw with Hazelnut Dressing

Mellowing out raw bitter greens such as kale and mustard greens is as simple as giving them a good massage to release enzymes that reduce the bitter-tasting compounds. Kohlrabi has a wonderful crisp flesh with a flavor reminiscent of broccoli and apple. It's stellar shredded and added to salads and slaws. The hazelnut dressing offers buttery notes, while the fruits provide a touch of sweetness.   *Serves 6   V, G, L*

1 medium kohlrabi, peeled and shredded (about 1 cup)

¼ teaspoon plus ⅛ teaspoon sea salt, divided

6 cups kale (about ½ bunch)

⅓ cup whole hazelnuts

2 tablespoons cider vinegar

1 teaspoon grated orange zest

1 teaspoon grainy mustard

2 teaspoons fresh thyme

1 clove garlic, minced

¼ teaspoon freshly ground black pepper

⅓ cup extra virgin olive oil

1 large red or orange bell pepper, thinly sliced

2 medium carrots, peeled and shredded

2 medium apples or pears, thinly sliced

⅓ cup dried cranberries or cherries

Parmesan cheese, shaved (optional)

Place the kohlrabi in a small bowl, toss with ⅛ teaspoon of the salt and let sit 10 minutes. Squeeze out as much water as possible and set aside.

Fold each leaf of kale in half lengthwise and slice out the center rib. Discard the ribs. Roll a stack of the leaves and slice in half lengthwise, then crosswise into very fine ribbons. Add to a large bowl.

Place the hazelnuts, cider vinegar, orange zest, mustard, thyme, garlic, remaining ¼ teaspoon salt, pepper, and olive oil in a food processor or blender container, and blend until well combined but still slightly chunky.

Toss together the kale and hazelnut dressing. With clean hands, firmly massage the greens for about 1 minute, or until tender. Add the kohlrabi, bell pepper, carrot, apple or pear, and dried cranberries or cherries to the kale, and toss to mix. Place on serving plates and garnish with shaved Parmesan if desired.

Top: KALE SLAW WITH HAZELNUT DRESSING, *page 52*

Bottom: CANTALOUPE PROSCIUTTO SKEWERS, *page 54*

Cantaloupe Prosciutto Skewers

These lively skewers are well suited for a summer backyard soirée. If fresh figs are available, don't miss the opportunity to include them. If they're not in season, you can try using dried figs.   *Serves 6 to 12   G*

1 small cantaloupe

Juice of 1 lime

2 tablespoons finely chopped mint

12 thin slices prosciutto (about 6 ounces), cut in half lengthwise

⅓ cup arugula

4 ounces bocconcini balls (about 1 cup), sliced in half, or fresh mozzarella cut into 1-inch cubes

3 fresh figs, sliced into wedges (optional)

12 (6-inch) wooden skewers

Slice the cantaloupe flesh into 1-inch cubes or use a melon baller to scoop it into balls. In a medium bowl, toss the cantaloupe with the lime juice and mint.

Thread one piece of cantaloupe and one piece of prosciutto onto a skewer followed by a few leaves of arugula. Finish by threading on one piece of cheese and a fig wedge if using. Repeat until you have two of each item on the skewer. Repeat with the remaining skewers.

Tofu Caprese Stacks

This riff on caprese salad replaces mozzarella with soft tofu. The results are wonderfully appetizing. Arugula pesto (see Smoked Salmon Arugula Pesto Sandwiches, page 78) is also a great option for this recipe, but you can use store-bought in a pinch.   *Serves 4   V, G*

Pesto:

1 cup packed fresh basil

2 cloves garlic, chopped

¼ cup walnut pieces

⅓ cup grated Parmigiano Reggiano or Parmesan cheese

Juice of ½ lemon

¼ teaspoon sea salt

¼ cup extra virgin olive oil

Caprese Stacks:

2 medium tomatoes, sliced into ½-inch rounds

8 ounces soft tofu, drained and sliced into ½-inch thick squares

⅓ cup prepared pesto (use the recipe here or store-bought)

1 tablespoon balsamic vinegar

¼ teaspoon freshly ground black pepper

To make the pesto, place the basil, garlic, and walnuts in the bowl of a food processor and pulse a few times until coarsely minced. Add the cheese, lemon juice, and salt, and process until combined. Scrape the sides of the bowl. Through the feed tube while the machine is running, slowly add the olive oil until fully combined.

To make the caprese stacks, top a slice of tomato with a one of the tofu squares and a dollop of pesto. Repeat with another slice of tomato, another square of tofu, and an additional dollop of pesto. Top with a third slice of tomato. Garnish with balsamic vinegar and pepper. Repeat with the remaining tomato, tofu, pesto, vinegar, and pepper.

Mango Spring Rolls with Almond Dipping Sauce

Handy Vietnamese rice paper wrappers are ideal for making refreshing and chic-looking appetizer or light lunch rolls. The nutty dipping sauce ups the ante on an already great dish. Carrots or cucumber are good fillings, as well. Or include frozen and thawed cooked shrimp or even smoked salmon to make this more of a main dish.   *Serves 8*   *V, G, L*

Spring Rolls:

2 ounces dried rice vermicelli noodles, preferably brown rice

16 round rice paper wrappers

1 large mango, peeled and cut into strips

1 small red bell pepper, thinly sliced

1 medium avocado, thinly sliced

16 fresh mint leaves, sliced in half

Dipping Sauce:

¼ cup unsalted almond butter

¼ cup coconut milk

2 teaspoons grated or finely minced fresh ginger

2 cloves garlic, grated or finely minced

2 tablespoons reduced-sodium soy sauce

2 tablespoons rice vinegar

1 teaspoon honey

2 teaspoons chili sauce, such as Sriracha

For the spring rolls: Bring 4 cups water to a boil using an electric kettle. Place the rice vermicelli noodles in a large heatproof bowl and pour the boiled water over the top. Allow the noodles to soak for 3 minutes. Drain and rinse under cold water. Place the noodles on a cutting board and slice into thirds so the noodles are about 2 inches long.

Fill a skillet or shallow pan with hot water; the pan should be large enough so the rice papers can lie flat. Fully submerge one rice paper wrapper in the water and soak until softened, about 20 seconds. Lay the softened wrapper flat on a cutting board or other clean work surface. Place a small bunch of vermicelli noodles in the bottom one-third of the wrapper, leaving about 1-inch free along the bottom edge. Lay three strips of mango, two strips of red pepper, and one slice of avocado over the noodles. Top with about 4 mint halves. Begin tightly rolling the wrapper and filling away from you. Fold in the left and right sides of the wrapper. Finish rolling tightly, and slice in half on the bias. Repeat with the remaining rice wrappers and filling.

For the dipping sauce: Whisk all the sauce ingredients together in a medium bowl until smooth. Serve the mango rolls with sauce on the side.

Top: MANGO SPRING ROLLS WITH ALMOND DIPPING SAUCE, *page 56*

Bottom: ZUCCHINI SMOKED FISH ROLLS, *page 58*

Zucchini Smoked Fish Rolls

These sophisticated rolls won't leave you fishing for compliments from tasters. They'll bring instant brightness to a party or any weeknight meal. Smoked fish like mackerel or salmon are well endowed with good-for-your-heart omega-3 fatty acids.   *Serves 4*   *G*

1 medium zucchini

½ cup packed flat-leaf parsley, finely chopped

2 tablespoons extra virgin olive oil

1 tablespoon lemon juice

¼ teaspoon freshly ground black pepper

4 ounces smoked mackerel, salmon, or trout, sliced into narrow strips

½ cup thinly sliced jarred roasted red pepper

Chop the ends off the zucchini and use a vegetable peeler or mandoline to slice the vegetable into long and wide thin strips. You want a total of 8 to 10.

In a small bowl, stir together the parsley, oil, lemon juice, and black pepper. Spread about ½ teaspoon of the parsley mixture on one of the zucchini strips, and place two slices of fish and two slices of red pepper at one end. Tightly roll up the zucchini strip and stab a toothpick through the middle to keep the roll together. Repeat with the remaining ingredients.

Broccoli with Cheesy Sauce

Don't get me wrong, I love good-quality cheese, but sometimes it's fun to try and re-create dishes with different types of food. Enter nutritional yeast. Available at most health food stores, the flakes have a flavor very reminiscent of cheese. They are also loaded with B vitamins and protein. The cashews give the not-so-cheesy sauce a creamy consistency. Often, I'll also blend in some chipotle chili powder, smoked paprika, or cayenne for a little kick. Placing broccoli florets in boiled water gives them a vibrant green color and soft texture similar to blanching, which involves cooking veggies briefly in a pot of boiling water on the stovetop. Also consider including peeled and thinly sliced tender broccoli stalks.   *Serves 4*   *V, G*

⅔ cup unsalted raw cashews

1 head of broccoli, coarsely chopped

⅓ cup nutritional yeast flakes

1 teaspoon garlic powder

1 teaspoon onion powder

½ teaspoon sea salt

¾ cup water

Place the cashews in a bowl of cold water and soak for 2 hours or more. Then drain the cashews and discard the water.

Place the broccoli florets in a large bowl. Bring a kettle full of water to a boil, pour over the broccoli, and let rest for 5 to 10 minutes, or until tender and bright green.

Meanwhile, place the cashews, nutritional yeast, garlic powder, onion powder, and salt in a blender container and add ¾ cup boiling water. Blend until smooth.

Drain the broccoli, place in a bowl, and top with the hot cheesy sauce.

Sunflower Tomato Pâté Nori Rolls

Packed with a wealth of nutrients, these quick nori rolls up the ante on snack time. The sunflower pâté can be made up to five days in advance to have on hand whenever you want to assemble a roll for a quick bite.   *Serves 8   V, G, L*

1 cup unsalted raw or roasted shelled sunflower seeds

½ cup oil-packed sun-dried tomatoes

2 tablespoons water

2 shallots, minced

2 cloves garlic, minced

Juice of ½ lemon

½ teaspoon sea salt

¼ teaspoon cayenne

¼ cup flat-leaf parsley

8 nori sheets

1 medium red bell pepper, thinly sliced

Place the sunflower seeds in a bowl, cover with cold water, and soak for 4 hours.

Drain the sunflower seeds and add them to a food processor container along with the remaining ingredients except parsley, nori, and bell pepper. Process until a pastelike texture forms, making sure to wipe down the container sides with a spatula a couple of times throughout. Add the parsley and pulse a few times to incorporate it into the spread.

Lay a nori sheet, rough side up, on a cutting board. Spread some of the sunflower mixture over the bottom half of the sheet and top with a few slices of bell pepper. Start rolling the nori sheet and filling away from you as tightly as possible. Moisten the top edge of the sheet with some water to help seal the roll. Slice in half or quarters to serve. Repeat with the remaining nori sheets, sunflower mixture, and bell pepper.

Top: SUNFLOWER TOMATO PÂTÉ NORI ROLLS, *page 60*

Bottom: CREAM CHEESE CRACKERS WITH SMOKED OYSTERS, *page 62*

Cream Cheese Crackers with Smoked Oysters

Smoked oysters are often overlooked in the canned fish aisle. Yet, their salty-chewy-smoky flavor is the perfect foil for crunchy crackers. Impress a crowd by serving this dish at your next shindig or enjoy it as a light lunch. Available in the Latin section of grocery stores, pickled jalapeño chile peppers provide a little fiery kick. You could also try a dash of hot sauce on top.   *Serves 6*

⅔ cup cream cheese, reduced-fat if desired

2 tablespoons dry white wine

1 tablespoon chopped chives

1 clove garlic, grated or very finely minced

1 tablespoon lemon juice

¼ teaspoon sea salt

¼ teaspoon freshly ground black pepper

12 crackers of choice, preferably thin-style

2 tins smoked oysters

¼ cup sliced pickled jalapeño chile peppers

In a medium bowl, stir together the cream cheese, white wine, chives, garlic, lemon juice, salt, and black pepper.

Spread the cream cheese mixture on the crackers and top with smoked oysters (about two per cracker) and sliced chile peppers.

Very Veggie Juice

With just a bit of chopping and a quick whirl you can have vegetable juice that tastes way better than store-bought and is brimming with disease-thwarting antioxidants. It's surprisingly filling and can stand alone as a mid-afternoon snack that will instantly make you feel years younger. If you want a thinner consistency, you can blend in some more water prior to serving.   *Serves 4   V, G, L*

1 cup water

3 medium tomatoes (about 1 pound), quartered

1 celery stalk, sliced

1 medium carrot, peeled and chopped

1 medium green bell pepper, chopped

½ small yellow onion, diced, or 2 green onions (scallions), white and green parts, sliced

⅓ cup flat-leaf parsley

1 clove garlic, chopped

Juice of ½ lemon

1½ teaspoons prepared horseradish

½ teaspoon sea salt

Few dashes of hot sauce such as Tabasco (optional)

Place all the ingredients in a blender or food processor container, and blend until smooth, about 1 minute. Taste and adjust seasoning as needed. Refrigerate for at least 2 hours before serving.

Very Berry Parfait Pudding

Here's a simple yet classy guilt-free snack that's chockablock with disease-fighting antioxidants, courtesy of the berry pudding. The pudding can be made up to five days in advance. Garnish options include grated dark chocolate, fresh mint, and whole berries. If speed is more important than presentation, simply stir together the pudding, yogurt, and granola in a bowl. *Serves 4 to 5   V, L*

2 cups fresh or frozen and thawed mixed berries such as blueberries, raspberries, and currants

10 ounces soft tofu (about 1 container)

2 tablespoons honey or agave syrup

1 teaspoon grated orange zest or lemon zest

½ teaspoon almond extract

1½ cups plain, low-fat yogurt

2 teaspoons vanilla extract

1 cup granola of choice

Place the berries, tofu, sweetener, citrus zest, and almond extract in a blender or food processor container and blend until smooth. Don't overprocess as you want the mixture to be slightly thick.

In a medium bowl, stir together the yogurt and vanilla extract.

To assemble a parfait, place some of the granola on the bottom of a parfait or other glass of choice and top with the yogurt followed by the berry pudding. Repeat so you have two layers of each.

Top: VERY BERRY PARFAIT PUDDING, *page 64*

Bottom: CHEESE DATE BALLS, *page 66*

Cheese Date Balls

One thing's for certain: These gourmet-looking and -tasting cheese balls will be a hit at any picnic, potluck, or other foodie gathering. The nut coating provides a pleasing crunchy contrast to creamy Brie cheese. Choose a Brie that's highly flavorful so the balls pop in your mouth.   *Serves 6 to 12   V, G, L*

⅓ cup shelled unsalted pistachios

⅓ cup unsalted raw or roasted almonds

10 ounces Brie cheese, room temperature

½ cup pitted and chopped dates

3 tablespoons white wine (optional)

1 shallot, chopped

1 teaspoon orange zest or lemon zest

¼ teaspoon sea salt

Place the pistachios and almonds in the bowl of a food processor, and process into small bits, but not to the point of turning them into dust. Place the processed nuts on a flat plate.

Add the remaining ingredients to the food processor container and blend until well combined. Form the cheese mixture into 12 balls a little smaller than golf balls. Roll the cheese balls in the nut mixture until the entire surface is covered. Refrigerate until firm, about 2 hours. Serve chilled or at room temperature.

Jerky Trail Mix

Who says trail mix has to be about just peanuts and raisins? You certainly don't have to be lost in the woods to enjoy this souped-up version featuring a little pow from wasabi peas and savory, chewy goodness courtesy of jerky. There are now a number of companies offering organic, MSG-free jerky ranging from beef to buffalo to turkey. Ideally, look for bags of popcorn with no more than three ingredients: popcorn, oil (not hydrogenated) or butter, and salt.   *Serves 8   G, L*

4 cups bagged popped popcorn

3 ounces coarsely chopped jerky of choice

1 cup coarsely chopped pecans

½ cup unsalted raw or roasted whole cashews

½ cup halved Brazil nuts

½ cup wasabi peas

½ cup dried cranberries, cherries, or blueberries

½ cup sliced dried apricots

⅓ cup unsalted pumpkin seeds

⅓ cup unsalted shelled sunflower seeds

Place all the ingredients in a large container and toss to combine. Store in a sealed airtight container or zip-top storage bag.

Chips and Dips

Here is a trio of flavorful and waistline-friendly dips for game day, parties, and other get-togethers. Serve with baked tortilla chips or sliced veggies, or even use them as sandwich spreads.

Chipotle Roasted Red Pepper Hummus

1 (14-ounce) can chickpeas, rinsed and drained

1 cup jarred roasted red pepper

2 cloves garlic, minced

3 tablespoons extra virgin olive oil

2 tablespoons tahini

Juice of ½ large lemon

2 teaspoons minced chipotle chile pepper in abodo sauce

½ teaspoon sea salt

¼ teaspoon freshly ground black pepper

Place all the ingredients in a food processor container and blend until smooth. Taste and add more chipotle if a hotter dip is desired. It will tend to get hotter after sitting for a day or two.

Guaca-mame

1½ cups frozen and thawed, shelled edamame

1 large ripe avocado

½ cup packed cilantro

⅓ cup plain low-fat yogurt

¼ cup packed fresh mint

2 tablespoons extra virgin olive oil

2 cloves garlic, minced

Grated zest of 1 lime

Juice of ½ lime

½ teaspoon ground cumin

½ teaspoon sea salt

¼ teaspoon cayenne (optional)

Place all the ingredients in a food processor container and blend until slightly chunky.

Tex-Mex Dip

½ cup unsalted pumpkin seeds
   (pepitas)

1 (14-ounce) can fat-free refried beans

4 ounces grated sharp cheddar cheese
   (about 1 cup)

½ cup jarred salsa of choice

½ cup low-fat sour cream

1 jalapeño chile pepper, seeded and
   minced

½ cup packed cilantro

Juice of ½ lemon

½ teaspoon ground cumin

½ teaspoon sea salt

Place the pumpkin seeds in a food processor container and process until reduced to small bits. Add the remaining ingredients and blend until well combined.

Main Dishes

When temperatures are soaring or time is not on your side, you might be tempted to dial for take-out instead of slaving over the stove. But you don't have to settle for eating a sodium tsunami pizza or Chinese fast food full of neon mystery sauces. Instead, assemble your meals with these no-cook suggestions, which are full of big flavors and nutritional bell ringers. Can't stand the heat? Start the cooling-off process with Peach Salad with Chocolate Vinaigrette (page 108) or satisfying Smoked Mackerel Subs with Cucumber Salsa (page 81). Not all no-cook meals have to be served cold, as shown by Green Tea Chicken Noodle Soup (page 88) and Asian-inspired Tofu Mushroom Miso Soup (page 95). You see, oven-free main dishes don't have to be just about humdrum salads. It's all about getting creative with precooked items like salami and canned lentils as a tasty way to neglect your pots and pans and help you stay cool and satisfied.

Shrimp Tacos with Tomatillo Black Bean Salsa

The tart, apple-flavored flesh of the tomatillo punches up this light and refreshing version of the famed Mexican condiment pico de gallo. You can change up the salsa by swapping out the pineapple for cantaloupe or mango. In lieu of shrimp, consider using canned tuna or rotisserie chicken.

Serves 4   G (if using 100% corn tortillas)

Salsa:

2 cups diced tomatillo

1 cup cubed pineapple

1 cup canned black beans, rinsed and drained

½ small red onion, finely diced

1 jalapeño chile pepper, seeded and minced

2 cloves garlic, minced

½ cup chopped cilantro

Juice of 1 lime

½ teaspoon ground cumin

¼ teaspoon sea salt

Tacos:

½ pound frozen and thawed cooked shrimp

8 (6 to 8-inch) corn or whole wheat tortillas

For the salsa: In a large bowl, toss together the tomatillo, pineapple, black beans, onion, chile pepper, garlic, cilantro, lime juice, cumin, and salt.

For the tacos: Divide the shrimp among the tortillas and top with the salsa.

Shrimp and Noodles with Sweet and Sour Sauce

Reminiscent of pad thai, this no-fuss noodle dish is sure to be awarded two chopsticks up by tasters. It's also the perfect option to combat a harried weeknight or when in need of healthy workday lunches. Be sure to use the wider rice noodles as opposed to the very thin vermicelli-style ones. More nutritious brown or red rice versions, such as those from Thai Kitchen, are now available in the Asian sections of grocery stores. Tamarind, a fruit often sold as a pulpy cake in Asian and Indian groceries, is used as a souring agent in cooking. Also consider tossing sugar snap peas into this dish.   *Serves 4 to 6   G, L*

½ box (about 8 ounces) wide Thai rice noodles

2 tablespoons chopped tamarind pulp or rice vinegar

2 tablespoons reduced-sodium soy sauce or tamari

1½ tablespoons fish sauce

1 tablespoon sesame oil

1 tablespoon coconut palm sugar, brown sugar, or honey

1 clove garlic, finely minced

1-inch piece fresh ginger or galangal, finely minced

2 dried Thai bird chile peppers, crushed or ¼ teaspoon dried red chili flakes

2 medium carrots, peeled and sliced into thin matchsticks

2 green onions (scallions), white and green parts, thinly sliced

2 cups bean sprouts

1 pound medium or large cooked frozen shrimp, thawed and shelled

⅓ cup coarsely chopped unsalted roasted peanuts

¼ cup coarsely chopped cilantro or Thai basil

1 lime, sliced into wedges

Place the noodles in a large heatproof bowl. Bring a full kettle of water to a boil and then pour over the noodles until fully covered. Let stand, stirring occasionally, until the noodles soften and become tender, 20 to 25 minutes. Drain well and place the noodles back in the bowl.

Meanwhile, if using tamarind place the pulp in a small bowl and mix with 4 tablespoons very hot water. Let soak for 10 minutes. Mash the tamarind with the back of a fork in the soaking water, press the mixture through a fine-mesh sieve, and reserve the tamarind water. Stir together the tamarind water or rice vinegar with the soy sauce, fish sauce, sesame oil, sweetener, garlic, ginger, and chile pepper. Add the dressing to the noodles and toss to coat. Taste and adjust seasonings as desired.

Add the carrot, green onion, and bean sprouts to the noodles and toss to combine. Divide the noodle mixture among serving plates, and top with the shrimp, peanuts, and cilantro or basil. Serve with lime wedges.

Tuna Radicchio Cups

Fennel has a distinct licorice flavor and crunchy texture, making it an exciting substitute for celery in tuna salad. Using radicchio as the wrap adds vibrant punch, but the tuna mixture is also great stuffed into pitas with some salad greens. As always, try to use sustainable canned tuna such as Wild Planet.   *Serves 4   G*

2 (5-ounce) cans albacore tuna, drained

½ cup plain, low-fat Greek yogurt or
low-fat mayonnaise

1 cup finely chopped fennel fronds
reserved for garnish

1 cup coarsely chopped parsley

⅓ cup raisins

1 tablespoon capers (optional)

1 teaspoon grated lemon zest

Juice of ½ lemon

1 teaspoon ground coriander

1 teaspoon paprika

¼ teaspoon sea salt

¼ teaspoon freshly ground black
pepper

8 radicchio leaves

Place the tuna in a large bowl and break apart the meat with a fork. Stir in the remaining ingredients except for the radicchio.

Divide the tuna mixture among the radicchio leaves and garnish with fennel fronds if desired.

Tuna Tartare with Avocado Mousse and Tomato Broth

If you're looking for a fanciful dish requiring not a lot of effort to serve dinner guests who are sushi lovers, this one won't disappoint. Make sure that your fishmonger is confident his or her tuna steaks are up to the task of being served raw. And really try to use wasabi in the avocado topping for a little extra punch.   *Serves 4*   *G*

Broth:

¾ pound tomatoes (about 3 medium), quartered

½ English cucumber, peeled and chopped

2 cloves garlic, minced

2 tablespoons red wine vinegar

1 tablespoon honey

¼ teaspoon sea salt

¼ teaspoon freshly ground black pepper

⅛ teaspoon cayenne

Tartare:

1 pound sushi-grade tuna, cut into ⅛-inch cubes

2 tablespoons extra virgin olive oil

Grated zest of 1 lime

Juice of 1 lime

1 teaspoon grated or finely minced ginger

¼ teaspoon sea salt

¼ teaspoon freshly ground black pepper

Mousse:

1 large ripe avocado

Juice of ½ lime

½ teaspoon wasabi powder (optional)

¼ teaspoon sea salt

2 tablespoons extra-virgin olive oil

2 tablespoons chopped chives, for garnish

For the broth: Place the tomato, cucumber, garlic, vinegar, honey, salt, black pepper, and cayenne in a blender container and blend until smooth, about 1 minute. Strain the tomato puree into a bowl using a wooden spoon to press the mixture through a fine sieve to remove any seeds. Refrigerate for at least 1 hour before serving.

For the tartare: In a bowl, toss together the tuna, olive oil, lime zest, lime juice, ginger, salt, and black pepper. Refrigerate for 1 hour before serving.

For the mousse: Place the avocado flesh, lime juice, wasabi powder if using, and salt in a blender or food processor container and blend until smooth. Add 1 tablespoon of water at a time if the mixture is too thick. With the machine running, drizzle in the olive oil until combined. Cover and refrigerate until ready to use.

Working one serving at a time, stuff the tuna mixture to a depth of about 1½ inches into either a ring mold an 8-inch cookie cutter, a 1-cup stainless steel measuring cup, a ramekin, or an empty tin can cut open at both ends. Unmold into a shallow serving bowl and place the tomato broth around the tuna circle. If using a mold such as ramekin with only one open end, simple turn it upside down into the bowl and lightly tap to release the tuna. Top with avocado mousse and chives.

Salmon Mango Ceviche

Popular in Central and South American cuisine, ceviche is a method of "cooking" seafood by letting it marinate in citrus juices. Besides salmon, suitable swimmers include tuna, bay scallops, halibut, shrimp, and red snapper, but it's always best to query your fishmonger about the freshest catch of the day. If you're watching your carb intake, you can replace the tortillas with lettuce wraps.   *Serves 4*   G

12 ounces very fresh skinless salmon, cut into ½-inch pieces

⅓ cup fresh lime juice

⅓ cup fresh lemon juice

⅓ cup fresh orange juice

1 medium avocado, diced

1 medium mango, cubed

1 large tomato, diced

½ cup finely diced red onion

1 jalapeño chile pepper, seeded and minced

2 tablespoons extra virgin olive oil

⅓ cup chopped cilantro

¼ teaspoon sea salt

8 (6 to 8-inch) corn tortillas

1 lime, sliced into wedges

In a large zip-top food storage bag, combine the salmon with the citrus juices. Allow to marinate in the refrigerator for a minimum of 4 hours and up to 8 hours, turning the bag a couple of times to mix. Drain the salmon and discard the liquid. Put the fish in a large bowl and add the avocado, mango, tomato, onion, chile pepper, olive oil, cilantro, and salt; stir gently to combine. Serve on corn tortillas with lime wedges for squirting on top.

Top: SALMON MANGO CEVICHE, *page 76*

Bottom: SMOKED SALMON ARUGULA PESTO SANDWICHES, *page 78*

Smoked Salmon Arugula Pesto Sandwiches

I love the peppery personality that arugula brings to pesto, the combination creating a flavor greater than the sum of its parts. You can certainly enjoy this robust sandwich at the office for lunch, but it's best to assemble it shortly before serving. The pesto can be made up to five days in advance. *Serves 4*

Pesto:

2 cups packed arugula

½ cup packed fresh basil

2 cloves garlic, chopped

½ cup chopped walnuts

1 ounce grated Parmesan or Parmigiano Reggiano (about ½ cup)

Juice of ½ lemon

¼ teaspoon sea salt

⅓ cup extra virgin olive oil or avocado oil

Sandwiches:

8 slices whole grain bread or 4 whole grain buns, split in half

4 ounces smoked salmon

½ English cucumber, thinly sliced

½ cup thinly sliced jarred roasted red pepper

½ cup sprouts, such as broccoli or pea (optional)

For the pesto: Place the arugula, basil, garlic, and walnuts in the bowl of a food processor and pulse a few times until coarsely minced. Add the cheese, lemon juice, and salt, and process until combined. Scrape the sides of the bowl. With the machine running, pour in the oil through the feed tube and blend until fully combined.

For the sandwiches: Spread a generous spoonful of pesto on four slices of bread or bun halves, and top with equal amounts of salmon, cucumber, red pepper, and sprouts if using. Top with the remaining bread or bun slices.

Salmon Lentil Stuffed Tomatoes with Curry Sauce

Salmon and lentils, a familiar combo in French bistro cooking, are stuffed into tomato cups for a wow presentation. You can use canned crab or tuna to stand in for salmon if desired. Instead of discarding the tomato innards, blend them into Very Veggie Juice (see page 63).   *Serves 4*   G

- 1 cup canned green lentils, rinsed and drained
- 1 (6-ounce) can salmon, drained or 1 (6-ounce) salmon pouch
- 1 celery stalk, thinly sliced
- 2 red radishes, diced
- 2 tablespoons capers (optional)
- Juice of ½ lemon plus 1 additional teaspoon fresh lemon juice, divided
- 1 clove garlic, minced
- 2 tablespoons chopped fresh dill
- 1–2 teaspoons Dijon mustard
- 1 teaspoon fennel seeds (optional)
- ¼ teaspoon sea salt
- ¼ teaspoon freshly ground black pepper
- 2 tablespoons extra virgin olive oil
- ½ cup plain, low-fat yogurt
- 1 teaspoon curry powder
- 4 large beefsteak tomatoes

In a large bowl, toss together the lentils, salmon, celery, radish, and capers if using.

In a small bowl, whisk together the juice of ½ lemon, garlic, dill, mustard, fennel seeds if using, salt, and pepper. Whisk in the olive oil. Add the olive oil mixture to the salmon and lentil mixture and combine gently. In a small bowl, stir together the yogurt, curry powder, and remaining 1 teaspoon lemon juice.

Slice ¼ inch off the tops of the tomatoes and guide a small knife around the interior. Use a spoon to scoop out the innards of each tomato. Fill the tomatoes with the salmon and lentil mixture and top with curry yogurt sauce.

Top: SALMON LENTIL STUFFED TOMATOES WITH CURRY SAUCE, *page 79*

Bottom: SMOKED MACKEREL SUBS WITH CUCUMBER SALSA, *page 81*

Smoked Mackerel Subs with Cucumber Salsa

Consider this a definite nutrition and flavor upgrade from the sloppy mayo-laden tuna salad at sub shops. Sustainable mackerel contains a boatload of must-have nutrients like omega-3 fatty acids and vitamin D. The recipe is just as good with smoked trout. If you're packing the sandwiches for lunch, keep the salad, salsa, and bun separate and assemble them right before eating to sidestep soggy bread. The subs also make for an easy make-ahead dinner.   *Serves 4*

Salsa:

1 English cucumber, peeled

½ cup finely diced red onion

⅓ cup chopped cilantro

¼ cup chopped fresh mint

1 jalapeño chile pepper, seeded and finely chopped

Juice of ½ lime

½ teaspoon ground cumin

¼ teaspoon sea salt

¼ teaspoon freshly ground black pepper

Salad:

1 pound smoked mackerel

½ cup reduced-fat sour cream

1 shallot, finely minced

1 clove garlic, finely minced

1 tablespoon white wine vinegar (optional)

2 teaspoons fresh lemon juice

2 tablespoons chopped fresh dill

1½ teaspoons prepared horseradish

4 (12-inch-long) baguettes or 4 ciabatta buns, preferably whole grain

2 tablespoons grainy Dijon mustard

For the salsa: Combine all the salsa ingredients in a large bowl and toss together.

For the salad: In a large bowl, remove the mackerel flesh from the skin and gently break it up with a fork. Add the sour cream, shallot, garlic, white wine vinegar if using, lemon juice, dill, and horseradish, and mix gently.

Slice the baguettes in half lengthwise or split the buns, and spread an equal amount of mustard on the bottom four slices. Top with the mackerel mixture, cucumber salsa, and remaining bread slices.

Rainbow Sardines on Rye

Wrongly chastised sardines contain an impressive amount of good stuff, including vitamin D, calcium, and heart-healthy omega-3 fats. You really get a huge nutrition bang for your buck. The flavors of brands vary greatly, so I always recommend trying a few different ones to see what pleases your palate the most. Make sure to use a good-quality, hearty rye bread. In the summer, I purchase rye loafs from the local German bakery and toast the slices right on my outdoor grill. You can also toast the slices in a toaster.   *Serves 4*

1 cup packed flat-leaf parsley

¾ cup oil-packed sun-dried tomatoes

2 cloves garlic, chopped

3 tablespoons extra virgin olive oil

2 tablespoons red wine vinegar

½ teaspoon sea salt

¼ teaspoon freshly ground black pepper

3 (4-ounce) cans water-packed sardines, drained

1 celery stalk, thinly sliced

½ cup finely diced red onion

1 small yellow or orange bell pepper, finely diced

1 small zucchini, shredded (about ½ cup)

⅓ cup chopped walnuts

¼ cup dried currants or golden raisins

8 slices rye bread

Sprouts, for garnish (optional)

Place the parsley, sun-dried tomatoes, garlic, oil, vinegar, salt, and black pepper in a food processor container, and blend until the tomatoes have broken down.

Place the sardines in a large bowl and break up the flesh gently with a fork. Fold in the celery, onion, bell pepper, zucchini, walnuts, and currants or raisins. Gently stir in the sun-dried tomato mixture.

Spread the sardine mixture on the bread slices and garnish with sprouts if desired.

Top: RAINBOW SARDINES ON RYE, *page 82*

Bottom: TUNA SALAD WITH WHITE BEAN DRESSING, *page 84*

Tuna Salad with White Bean Dressing

Influenced by Mediterranean flavors, this substantial salad is geared toward providing a rainbow of colors on your dinner plate. And from all those hues, you'll reap the full spectrum of antioxidants that Mother Nature provides. *Serves 4   G*

Salad:

6 cups leafy vegetables, such as lettuce, spinach, radicchio, and mesclun

1 large red or orange bell pepper, thinly sliced

1 cup halved cherry tomatoes

1 large avocado, thinly sliced

2 (5-ounce) cans albacore tuna, drained

⅓ cup pitted and sliced kalamata olives

2 tablespoons capers

Dressing:

1 cup canned white navy beans, rinsed and drained

½ cup plain, low-fat yogurt

1 cup packed flat-leaf parsley

2 tablespoons tahini

1 teaspoon Dijon mustard

Juice of ½ lemon

2 cloves garlic, finely chopped

¼ teaspoon sea salt

¼ teaspoon freshly ground black pepper

For the salad: In a large bowl, toss together the greens, bell pepper, cherry tomatoes, and avocado. Break the tuna meat into chunks with a fork. Divide the salad among serving plates, and top with the tuna chunks, olives, and capers.

For the dressing: Place all dressing ingredients in a blender or food processor container and blend until smooth. Taste and adjust seasonings as needed. Drizzle over the salad.

Mango Crab Salad

This fresh salad achieves the alluring combination of sweet, salty, sour, and bitter flavors. Crunchy unripe green mangoes can be easily grated and their wonderful tart flavor is a nice contrast to the delicate crab. You can find unripe green mangoes at most Chinese and other Asian groceries. Or you could substitute with green papaya or even a not-yet-ripe red-skinned, yellow-fleshed mango. If canned crab doesn't appeal to you, look for pasteurized ready-to-eat crabmeat in the refrigerator case at the fish counter.   *Serves 4   G, L*

1½ pounds green mango (about 3 fruits), peeled

½ English cucumber

2 (6-ounce) cans crabmeat, drained or 1 pound pasteurized fresh crabmeat

1 cup thinly sliced radish

2 cups halved cherry tomatoes

⅓ cup chopped watercress or cilantro

⅓ cup chopped fresh mint or basil

2 tablespoons fish sauce

1 tablespoon rice vinegar

1 tablespoon coconut palm sugar or honey

1 tablespoon sesame oil

2 cloves garlic, finely minced

2 teaspoons finely minced ginger

Juice of 1 lime

¼ teaspoon dried red chili flakes

Pea shoots or chopped chives, for garnish

Using a serrated vegetable peeler or box grater, shred the mango flesh, or, alternatively, julienne the mango very finely with a sharp knife. Place the shredded or julienned mango in a large bowl. Slice the cucumber in half lengthwise and use a small spoon to scrape out the seeds. Thinly slice the cucumber along its width and add the slices to the bowl with the mango. Add the crabmeat, radish, tomato, watercress or cilantro, and mint or basil. Toss the mixture together.

In a small bowl, whisk together the fish sauce, rice vinegar, sugar or honey, sesame oil, garlic, ginger, lime juice, and chili flakes.

Add the dressing to the mango mixture and toss to coat. Serve the salad garnished with pea shoots or chives.

Moroccan Chicken Salad

Make this highly textured salad on a lazy weekend afternoon and you'll be set for several exciting workday lunches or quick dinners. Couscous requires only boiling water to prepare. For added nutrition use a whole wheat version. *Ras el hanout* is the classic Moroccan seasoning used in couscous dishes. It often contains a laundry list of spices and herbs, so to simplify things I suggest using store-bought *ras el hanout*, which is available in well-stocked spice aisles or Middle Eastern markets. If you have them on hand, a few slices of preserved lemon are a wonderful addition. *Serves 4 to 6   L*

Salad:

1 cup water

1 cup couscous, preferably whole wheat

½ teaspoon saffron threads

¼ teaspoon sea salt

2 to 3 cups diced cooked rotisserie chicken

1 medium carrot, peeled and thinly sliced

1 cup halved cherry tomatoes

½ English cucumber, chopped

2 green onions (scallions), white and green parts, thinly sliced

¼ cup coarsely chopped fresh mint or cilantro

½ cup coarsely chopped dried apricots

⅓ cup unsalted slivered almonds

Dressing:

¼ cup extra virgin olive oil or almond oil

2 tablespoons ras el hanout spice mixture

1 teaspoon grated lemon zest

Juice of ½ lemon

For the salad: Bring water to a boil using an electric kettle. In a large heatproof bowl, stir 1 cup boiled water with the couscous, saffron, and salt. Cover and let stand until the water has been absorbed, about 5 minutes. Fluff couscous with a fork and let cool to room temperature.

Add the chicken, carrot, cherry tomatoes, cucumber, green onion, mint or cilantro, apricots, and almonds to the bowl with the couscous and stir to combine.

For the dressing: In a small bowl, whisk together the oil, ras el hanout, lemon zest, and lemon juice. Add the dressing to the couscous salad and stir to combine.

Top: MOROCCAN CHICKEN SALAD, *page 86*

Bottom: GREEN TEA CHICKEN NOODLE SOUP, *page 88*

Green Tea Chicken Noodle Soup

This no-simmering-required soup is good for sniffles and hungry bellies. A delightful green tea broth, store-bought cooked chicken, and rice noodles help make it happen minus the stove.   *Serves 4 to 6   G, L*

½ package (about 8 ounces) wide Thai rice noodles

4 green tea bags or 2 tablespoons loose leaf green tea

7 cups water, divided

2 to 3 cups shredded or finely chopped cooked rotisserie chicken

2 stalks celery, thinly sliced

2 medium carrots, peeled and thinly sliced

1 cup fresh, canned, or frozen and thawed green peas

2 green onions (scallions), white and green parts, thinly sliced

⅓ cup chopped flat-leaf parsley

2 teaspoons fresh thyme

½ teaspoon red chile flakes, or to heat tolerance

½ teaspoon sea salt

¼ teaspoon freshly ground black pepper, plus more for garnish

Place the noodles in a large heatproof bowl. Using an electric kettle, bring a full kettle of water to a boil and pour over the noodles until fully covered. Let stand, stirring occasionally, until the noodles soften and become tender, 20 to 25 minutes. Drain well and slice the noodles into 2-inch pieces.

Meanwhile, bring more water to a boil. Place 3 cups boiled water and the tea bags or loose leaf tea in a large saucepan, cover, and let steep 15 minutes. Remove the tea bags and discard. If using loose leaf tea, drain the water into a bowl, discard the tea leaves, and return the water to the saucepan. Bring additional water to a boil, and pour 4 cups into the saucepan with the tea infused liquid. Add the noodles along with the chicken, celery, carrot, peas, green onion, parsley, thyme, chile flakes, salt, and black pepper. Cover and let stand 5 minutes.

Ladle the soup into serving bowls and garnish with freshly ground black pepper.

BBQ Chicken Sandwiches with Pickled Vegetables

With the vinegary snap of the vegetable topping and rich fiery kick courtesy of the DIY barbecue sauce, you'd be hard pressed to find a sandwich more awash in flavor. Or one that can silence your hunger pangs any better. You can make the pickled vegetables and sauce up to two days in advance. Dried ancho chile peppers are sold in Latin markets and many natural food stores. If you can't locate them, substitute with about 2 teaspoons canned chipotle chile pepper in abodo sauce.   *Serves 6*

1¼ cups water, divided

1 cup white distilled vinegar

½ cup granulated sugar

2½ teaspoons sea salt, divided

1 teaspoon mustard seeds (optional)

4 cups thinly sliced red cabbage

1 small red onion, thinly sliced

2 dried ancho chile peppers

½ cup ketchup

2 shallots, chopped

2 cloves garlic, minced

2 tablespoons cider vinegar

1 tablespoon tomato paste

1 tablespoon molasses, not blackstrap

2 teaspoons Worcestershire sauce

½ teaspoon ground cumin

½ teaspoon ground allspice

¼ teaspoon freshly ground black
   pepper

4 cups shredded or finely chopped
   cooked rotisserie chicken

6 whole grain buns, split in half

To make the pickled vegetables, begin by bringing water to a boil using an electric kettle. In a large heatproof container or bowl, place the vinegar, sugar, 2 teaspoons salt, and mustard seeds if using. Pour in 1 cup boiled water and stir until the sugar has dissolved. Add the cabbage and red onion. Stir to combine, cover, and let stand for at least 2 hours at room temperature, stirring a couple of times.

Meanwhile, start the BBQ sauce by soaking the ancho chile peppers in very hot water for 15 minutes, or until soft. Slice off the stems, and remove and reserve the seeds. Place the chile peppers in a blender or food processor container along with as many seeds as you like. If you want a milder sauce, add only a few of the seeds or include more seeds if you want it fiery. Add the ketchup, ¼ cup water, shallots, garlic, cider vinegar, tomato paste, molasses, Worcestershire sauce, cumin, allspice, black pepper, and remaining ½ teaspoon salt, and blend until smooth. Add a little extra water if needed to help with blending.

Place the chicken in a bowl and toss with the barbecue sauce until all the meat is well coated. Divide the chicken among the bottom halves of the buns, and top with pickled vegetables and remaining bun halves.

Root Vegetable Salami Salad with Maple Vinaigrette

When sweater weather arrives, it's time to dig deep for root vegetables to make this salad. When sliced paper-thin, beets, celery root, and other seasonal roots are wonderful uncooked. Try to use smaller roots since they will be sweeter tasting. For added splash, I like to use golden and candy cane beets. But if using red beets, add them to the salad just before serving to keep their color from bleeding into the other vegetables.

Serves 6   V, G, L

Salad:

½ pounds beets (about 4 medium)

2 carrots, peeled

1 small celery root (celeriac), peeled

1 small daikon radish or 6 red radishes

1 bunch broccoli stalks, peeled to the tender white flesh (optional)

2 oranges or 6 mandarin oranges

6 cups mixed greens, such as spinach, arugula, and mesclun

1 (14-ounce) can chickpeas, rinsed and drained

6 ounces salami or summer sausage, chopped

4 ounces feta cheese (about 1 cup), diced

⅓ cup chopped walnuts

Dressing:

2 tablespoons pure maple syrup

2 tablespoons red wine vinegar

1 to 2 teaspoons Dijon mustard

¼ teaspoon sea salt

¼ teaspoon freshly ground black pepper

¼ cup extra virgin olive oil

For the salad: Using a vegetable peeler, mandoline, or razor-sharp knife, very thinly slice the beets, carrots, celery root, radish, and broccoli stalks if using. Place the sliced vegetables in a large bowl and toss to mix. Separate the oranges or mandarins into segments and slice each into thirds.

Divide the greens among serving plates and top with the vegetable mixture. Top the salad with orange pieces, chickpeas, salami or sausage, feta, and walnuts.

For the dressing: In a small bowl, whisk together the maple syrup, vinegar, mustard, salt, and pepper. Whisking constantly, slowly add the oil. Drizzle the maple dressing over the salad.

Pizza Stacks

Pizza, meet the sandwich. A fun twist to pizza night, indeed. Place all the toppings on the table and let everyone build their own. Another protein option is cooked rotisserie chicken. Sweet and slightly hot Peppadew chile peppers are available at many supermarket deli counters, but roasted red peppers are a good substitute. And if not using anchovies, which provide a savory, salty kick to the pizza sauce, blend in about ¼ teaspoon sea salt.   *Serves 4*

¼ cup extra virgin olive oil

10 oil-packed sun-dried tomatoes

6 Peppadew chile peppers

3 canned anchovy fillets (optional)

¼ cup packed fresh basil

2 cloves garlic, chopped

2 tablespoons fresh oregano or
  1 teaspoon dried oregano

¼ teaspoon cayenne or chili powder

8 whole grain sandwich thins

⅓ pound thinly sliced pepperoni or
  salami such as soppressata

⅓ cup sliced jarred artichoke hearts

⅓ cup sliced olives of choice

1 small yellow bell pepper, thinly sliced

¼ cup sliced jarred pickled jalapeño
  chile peppers (optional)

2 cups arugula or baby spinach

4 ounces grated mozzarella cheese
  (about 1 cup)

Place the olive oil, sun-dried tomatoes, Peppadew chile peppers, anchovies if using, basil, garlic, oregano, and cayenne or chili powder in a food processor or blender container, and blend until slightly chunky.

Toast the bottom halves of the bread. Spread the tomato sauce on the toasted bread and top with the remaining ingredients, making sure to place the cheese on top. Toast the other halves of the bread and place them on top of the cheese. The cheese will slightly melt from the heat of the toasted bread.

Top: PIZZA STACKS, *page 92*
Bottom: ROAST BEEF WRAPS, *page 94*

Roast Beef Wraps

Surprising to many, roast beef is generally one of the leanest options at the deli counter, and Asian chefs often refer to thick and tangy hoisin sauce as the Chinese barbecue sauce. In this recipe, hoisin sauce is the starting point for a tangy, rich spread for the wraps. The sauce also features Chinese five spice, an undervalued addition to sauces consisting of star anise, Szechwan pepper, cloves, Chinese cinnamon, and fennel seeds. Use any extra sauce for dipping the tortillas. *Serves 4* *L*

Sauce:

⅓ cup hoisin sauce

2 tablespoons honey

1½ tablespoons soy sauce

1½ teaspoons Chinese five spice powder

1 clove garlic, grated or very finely minced

Grated zest of 1 lemon

¼ teaspoon freshly ground black pepper

⅛ teaspoon cayenne, or to taste

Wraps:

4 large (12-inch) whole grain tortilla wraps

2 cups greens such as baby spinach, watercress, or arugula

½ pound thinly sliced roast beef

1 cup sliced jarred roasted red pepper

1 cup sprouts such as broccoli, alfalfa, or onion (optional)

For the sauce: In a medium bowl, whisk together the hoisin sauce, honey, soy sauce, Chinese five spice powder, garlic, lemon zest, black pepper, and cayenne.

For the wraps: Lay the tortillas flat on a work surface and spread the hoisin mixture over the entire surface of each. Top with an equal amount of greens, roast beef, roasted red pepper, and sprouts if using. Tightly roll up the tortillas, insert a toothpick at each end, and slice the wraps in half on the bias. Serve immediately or refrigerate for later use.

Tofu Mushroom Miso Soup

This Japanese-inspired healthy soup is best enjoyed with chopsticks and bowl-to-mouth slurping. Silken firm tofu is a soft-type tofu available in shelf-stable boxes that has some body to it so it's not completely pudding-like. Miso is considered a "live" food since it's fermented and harbors beneficial bacteria the same way yogurt does. It also adds tempered saltiness, while the dried mushrooms give the soup a meaty texture. For the best prices, I'll source my miso, mushrooms, bok choy, and seaweed from an Asian grocery store. Because I like my soup to have a little kick, I stir in a whisper of hot sauce at the table.   *Serves 4 to 6   V (if omitting fish sauce), G, L*

1 cup sliced dried mushrooms

6 cups water, divided

4 tablespoons miso paste

1 tablespoon sesame oil

1 tablespoon fish sauce (optional)

12 ounces (1 block) silken firm tofu, cut into ½-inch pieces

6 baby bok choy, trimmed at the base and thinly sliced

1 large carrot, peeled and sliced into thin matchsticks

6 thin slices peeled fresh ginger

2 green onions (scallions), white and green parts, thinly sliced

2 crumbled nori sheets or ¼ cup dried wakame flakes

2 teaspoons sesame seeds

Asian hot sauce like Sriracha or sambal oelek (optional)

Place the mushrooms in a bowl, cover with cold water, and soak until softened, about 30 minutes. Drain and set aside.

Using an electric kettle, bring a full kettle of water to just under a boil. If you have a small kettle, you can do this in batches. Place the miso and 1½ cups boiled water in a small heatproof bowl and whisk until the miso dissolves. Add the dissolved miso to a large heatproof bowl or saucepan along with the remaining 4½ cups boiled water, mushrooms, sesame oil, fish sauce if using, tofu, bok choy, carrot, ginger, green onion, and nori or wakame. Cover and let stand 3 minutes before serving.

Ladle the soup into serving bowls and garnish with sesame seeds. If desired, stir in a little hot sauce.

Top: TOFU MUSHROOM MISO SOUP, *page 95*

Bottom: NO-FRY TOFU BROCCOLI STIR-FRY, *page 97*

No-Fry Tofu Broccoli Stir-Fry

Stirred but not fried is how you can describe this fresh-tasting and nutrient-packed dish, which is served on cauliflower "rice" for a whimsical twist. I always like to bring some heat to the table, so I top it all off with a few dashes of hot sauce. If you have them on hand, sprouts are a wonderful garnish.   *Serves 6   V, G, L*

1 block (about 1 pound) firm tofu

2 cups coarsely chopped broccoli
   florets

2 cups thinly sliced cremini mushrooms

2 cups snow peas, ends trimmed

2 medium carrots, peeled and sliced
   into matchsticks

½ cup unsalted raw or toasted cashews

⅓ cup neutral-tasting oil such as canola
   or grapeseed

2 tablespoons reduced-sodium soy
   sauce

2 tablespoons rice vinegar

1½ tablespoons sesame oil

1 tablespoon honey

2 cloves garlic, finely minced

1 tablespoon finely minced ginger

1 teaspoon Chinese five spice powder

½ teaspoon sea salt

¼ teaspoon red chile flakes

1 head cauliflower, coarsely chopped

Stand the tofu on end and slice in half lengthwise. Do the same for each tofu half. Slice the four pieces of tofu along their width into matchsticks. In a large bowl, toss together the tofu, broccoli, mushrooms, snow peas, carrot, and cashews.

In a medium bowl, whisk together the oil, soy sauce, vinegar, sesame oil, honey, garlic, ginger, Chinese five spice powder, salt, and chile flakes. Toss the dressing with the tofu mixture and let marinate for at least 2 hours in the refrigerator, stirring a couple of times.

In a food processor, pulse the chopped cauliflower until it resembles rice. You will most likely have to do this in batches.

To serve, divide the cauliflower among serving plates and top with the dressed tofu mixture.

Smoked Tofu Wraps

Smoked tofu and sun-dried tomatoes team up to create a dish even hardened meat lovers will be smitten with. Available alongside other tofu varieties, the smoked version has a wonderful meaty texture that shreds very easily. Wrapping the tofu-tomato mixture in a leafy green keeps the dish tasting fresher than when using flour wraps.   *Serves 4   V, G*

6 to 8 ounces smoked tofu (about 1 small block)

1 large carrot, peeled

1 small red bell pepper, chopped

2 green onions (scallions), white and green parts, thinly sliced

⅓ cup extra virgin olive oil

⅓ cup oil-packed sun-dried tomatoes

Juice of ½ lemon

1 clove garlic, minced

1 teaspoon paprika, preferably smoked

¼ teaspoon sea salt

¼ teaspoon freshly ground black pepper

8 Swiss chard or large lettuce leaves

In a large bowl, shred the tofu and carrot using a box grater or mandoline. Add the bell pepper and green onion, and toss the tofu mixture together.

Place the oil, sun-dried tomatoes, lemon juice, garlic, paprika, salt, and pepper in a blender or food processor container. Blend until well combined and just slightly chunky.

Divide the tofu mixture among the Swiss chard or lettuce leaves and top with the sun-dried tomato mixture. To eat, fold the leaves over taco-style.

Tex-Mex Chipotle Beans

Even if you've become blasé about bean salads, this Tex-Mex version will have you doling out second helpings. The fiber-packed dish makes for wonderful leftovers, but make sure to stir in the chips just before serving so they stay crunchy. Smoky-tasting chipotle chile peppers in adobo sauce are found in the Latin section of most grocers, but if unavailable you can use dried ancho or chipotle chili powder, smoked paprika, or minced jalapeño chile pepper for a little burn. If using frozen corn kernels, simply soak them in some boiled water for a few minutes before using. *V, G (if using gluten-free chips), L*

1 (14-ounce) can white navy beans, rinsed and drained

1 (14-ounce) can kidney beans, rinsed and drained

1 (14-ounce) can black beans, rinsed and drained

1 large red bell pepper, chopped

1 large avocado, diced

1 cup corn kernels, canned or frozen and thawed

¼ cup hemp seeds (optional)

1 pound tomatoes (about 3 medium), quartered

½ small red onion, finely diced (about ⅓ cup)

⅓ cup packed cilantro

1 tablespoon chopped chipotle chile pepper in adobo sauce, or to heat tolerance

1 clove garlic, chopped

Juice of ½ lime

1 teaspoon ground cumin

¼ teaspoon sea salt

¼ teaspoon freshly ground black pepper

½ cup reduced-fat sour cream

1 cup grated sharp cheddar cheese or pepper Jack cheese

1 cup coarsely crushed baked tortilla chips

In a large bowl, toss together the beans, bell pepper, avocado, corn, and hemp seeds if using.

Add the tomato, onion, cilantro, chipotle chile pepper, garlic, lime juice, cumin, salt, and black pepper to a blender or food processor container, and pulse until well combined but still slightly chunky. Pulse in the sour cream. Pour the tomato mixture over the beans and stir to coat. Stir in the cheese and tortilla chips. Serve at room temperature or chilled.

Top: TEX-MEX CHIPOTLE BEANS, *page 99*

Bottom: MEDITERRANEAN CHICKPEA PITAS WITH TAHINI DRESSING, *page 101*

Mediterranean Chickpea Pitas with Creamy Tahini Dressing

Here's a way to break out of the ham and cheese lunchtime sandwich doldrums. However, the chickpea mixture with serious nutritional firepower is equally good as a stand-alone salad without the pita. *Serves 4* *V*

1 (14-ounce) can chickpeas, rinsed and drained

1 small red bell pepper, diced

½ English cucumber, diced

2 Roma (plum) tomatoes, seeds removed and chopped

½ cup finely diced red onion

½ cup chopped cilantro or flat-leaf parsley

4 ounces cubed feta cheese (about 1 cup)

⅓ cup chopped black olives

¼ cup raisins

3 tablespoons extra virgin olive oil

2 tablespoons tahini

Juice of 1 lemon

2 cloves garlic, minced

½ teaspoon ground cumin

¼ teaspoon cayenne

¼ teaspoon sea salt

¼ teaspoon freshly ground black pepper

1 tablespoon water

4 (6-inch) whole grain pitas, sliced in half

In a large bowl, toss together the chickpeas, bell pepper, cucumber, tomato, red onion, cilantro or parsley, feta cheese, olives, and raisins.

Place the olive oil, tahini, lemon juice, garlic, cumin, cayenne, salt, black pepper, and water in a blender, and blend until smooth. Add the tahini mixture to the chickpea mixture and stir to coat.

To serve, stuff the chickpea mixture into pitas.

Oat Waldorf Salad

This update of Waldorf salad uses oats as a surprising addition. Soaking the grain overnight gives it a wonderful chewy texture. For the dressing, it's best to use traditional yogurt rather than the thicker Greek yogurt. Supermarket rotisserie chicken, canned salmon, and canned tuna are protein options instead of canned chicken or turkey. Be sure to mix in some parsley just before serving to freshen up the flavor, which only gets better after resting in the refrigerator for a day or two.   *Serves 6*   *V, L*

1 cup steel-cut oats

1½ cups water

2 (5-ounce) cans chicken or turkey breast meat

2 stalks celery, thinly sliced

1½ cups halved seedless red grapes

1 large apple, diced

½ cup chopped walnuts

½ cup plain, low-fat yogurt

2 tablespoons white wine vinegar or rice vinegar

1 teaspoon curry powder

½ teaspoon dry mustard powder (optional)

¼ teaspoon sea salt

¼ teaspoon freshly ground black pepper

Flat-leaf parsley, coarsely chopped, for garnish

Place the oats in a bowl or container and cover with the water. Let soak overnight or for several hours. Drain the oats and place them in a large container along with the chicken or turkey meat, celery, grapes, apple, and walnuts.

In a small bowl, whisk together the yogurt, vinegar, curry powder, mustard powder, salt, and black pepper. Add the yogurt mixture to the oat mixture and stir to coat.

Place the salad in serving bowls and garnish with parsley.

Bean Tacos with Cabbage Slaw

Creamy and crunchy at the same time, this dish is perfect for your next taco night. The recipe is pretty adaptable based on taste. For example, you can replace the sour cream with plain yogurt, hard tacos with soft ones, or pinto beans with black beans. Also try precooked shredded chicken instead of beans. The components can be made a day or two in advance as the flavors only improve with some time. *Serves 4* *V, G (if using 100% corn tacos)*

2 cups shredded or finely sliced red cabbage

1 cup shredded carrot

2 tablespoons rice vinegar

2 tablespoons sweet chili sauce, such as Thai Kitchen

2 tablespoons neutral-tasting oil such as canola or grapeseed

2 (15-ounce) cans pinto beans, rinsed and drained

1 large avocado, cubed

1 teaspoon ground cumin

2 green onions (scallions), white and green parts, thinly sliced

⅓ cup chopped cilantro

⅔ cup reduced-fat sour cream

¼ teaspoon chipotle or other chili powder

Juice of ½ lime

12 hard shell tacos

In a large bowl, toss together the cabbage and carrot. In a small bowl, whisk together the rice vinegar, chili sauce, and oil. Add the vinegar mixture to the cabbage mixture and toss to coat. Set aside.

In a separate bowl, toss together the beans, avocado, cumin, green onion, and cilantro. In another separate bowl, stir together the sour cream, chili powder, and lime juice. Taste and add more chili powder if desired.

Stuff each taco with bean mixture, and top with slaw and sour cream sauce.

Top: BEAN TACOS WITH CABBAGE SLAW, *page 103*

Bottom: LENTIL WILD RICE PILAF, *page 105*

Lentil Wild Rice Pilaf

This wild and wonderful riff on pilaf requires no cooking, just a little patience as you let the wild rice soak until it has a pleasant chewy texture. Truth be told, nutty-tasting wild rice isn't actually rice, but rather a nutritious aqueous grass traditionally harvested by Native peoples using canoes. If pomegranates aren't in season, simply use dried cranberries or dried cherries instead.   *Serves 6   V, G, L*

1 cup wild rice

2 (15-ounce) cans lentils, rinsed and drained

2 celery stalks, thinly sliced

1 large apple, diced

Seeds of 1 pomegranate

⅓ cup chopped walnuts or pecans

2 green onions (scallions), white and green parts, thinly sliced

2 tablespoons fresh marjoram or oregano

3 tablespoons extra virgin olive oil or walnut oil

2 tablespoons red wine vinegar

2 cloves garlic, finely minced

¼ teaspoon sea salt

¼ teaspoon freshly ground black pepper

¼ teaspoon red chile flakes

Place the wild rice in a glass container and cover with water. Let soak about 3 days, or until tender and chewy. Ideally, try and change the water once or twice daily.

In a large bowl, toss together the soaked wild rice, lentils, celery, apple, pomegranate seeds, nuts, green onion, and marjoram or oregano. In a small bowl, whisk together the oil, vinegar, garlic, salt, black pepper, and chile flakes. Add the dressing to the salad and toss to mix.

Shaved Squash Salad

Raw zucchini is usually not awarded many praises, but when shaved thinly it becomes a whole new vegetable. Chickpeas make this salad heartier, not to mention add a healthy dose of fiber, vitamins, and minerals. Toss in some squash blossoms and/or sprouts such as pea shoots if they're available. Garnish options include grated Parmesan, sesame seeds, and additional ground black pepper.   *Serves 4   G, V*

Salad:

1½ pounds zucchini (about 3 medium), preferably a mix of green and yellow

1 large red bell pepper, thinly sliced

1 (14-ounce) can chickpeas, rinsed and drained

1 cup halved cherry tomatoes

⅓ cup coarsely chopped fresh basil

2 ounces diced feta, goat, or blue cheese (about ½ cup)

⅓ cup chopped walnuts or pecans

Dressing:

¼ cup extra virgin olive or walnut oil

1 tablespoon red wine vinegar

1 to 2 teaspoons Dijon mustard

1 teaspoon honey

1 clove garlic, minced

¼ teaspoon sea salt

¼ teaspoon freshly ground black pepper

For the salad: Using a wide, flat vegetable peeler or mandoline, shave the squash thinly into a large bowl. Toss with the bell pepper, chickpeas, cherry tomatoes, and basil. Divide the squash mixture among serving plates and top with cheese and nuts.

For the dressing: In a small bowl, whisk together the dressing ingredients and drizzle over the salad.

Top: SHAVED SQUASH SALAD, *page 106*

Bottom: PEACH SALAD WITH CHOCOLATE VINAIGRETTE, *page 108*

Peach Salad with Chocolate Vinaigrette

Chocolate on a salad—who knew? Paired with peaches, peppery arugula, salty prosciutto, and crunchy almonds, it makes a praiseworthy salad. If desired, you can replace the spinach with endive and the mozzarella with soft goat cheese. If the vinaigrette solidifies upon sitting, whisk in an additional 1 tablespoon hot water.   *Serves 4   G*

Dressing:

2 ounces dark chocolate (about ½ cup), finely chopped

½ cup water

¼ cup extra virgin olive oil

1 tablespoon balsamic vinegar

2 teaspoons honey

1 teaspoon Dijon mustard

¼ teaspoon sea salt

Pinch of dried red chile flakes

Salad:

3 cups baby spinach

3 cups arugula

¼ cup fresh mint

2 ripe peaches, thinly sliced

2 ounces prosciutto, sliced

4 ounces fresh mozzarella, chopped (about ½ cup)

⅓ cup coarsely chopped almonds

⅓ cup dried cherries (optional)

For the dressing: Place the chocolate in a medium heatproof bowl. Bring water to a boil in an electric kettle and pour ½ cup over the chocolate, and let sit 10 minutes without stirring. Carefully drain as much water as possible from the bowl and immediately stir in the olive oil, vinegar, honey, mustard, salt, and chile flakes until smooth.

For the salad: In a large bowl, toss together the spinach, arugula, mint, and peaches. Divide the salad among serving plates and top with equal amounts of prosciutto, mozzarella, almonds, and cherries if using. Drizzle chocolate dressing over the top.

Desserts

Nothing is quite as comforting as taking a freshly baked pie out of the oven as the kitchen becomes redolent of its warming spices. But when you look out the window at waves of shimmering heat, the thought of baking a dessert is probably enough for you to lose your appetite. Thankfully, the summer is a wonderful time to take advantage of chilly treats that don't involve cranking up the temperature in your kitchen.

Some recipes like luscious Avocado Chocolate Mousse (page 117) and Individual Fruit Crisps with Vanilla-Scented Yogurt (page 125) are ideal if you're in need of a quick treat, but if you have a little more time on your hands, recipes such as Vanilla Ice Cream Cupcakes (page 132) and Cherry Granita (page 113) reward those who put in a bit of effort. By no means are all of these desserts appropriate only for the summer months. Applesauce Pie (page 139) and Almond Thumbprint Cookies (page 131) come to mind as tasty options for any season. Best of all, with the use of fresh fruits, crunchy nuts, and whole grains, most of these recipes also provide nutritional perks, making them even easier to swallow.

Banana Split with Banana Ice Cream

Here's a dessert that screams for one plate and two spoons. The frozen bananas along with coconut milk are simply blended and transformed into a smooth, velvety ice cream. If desired, you could leave out the coconut milk and replace it with a couple tablespoons of nut butter. Melting chocolate using boiled water is a trick I learned when developing a recipe for a campsite fondue.   *Serves 4   V, G*

3 large frozen bananas

½ cup coconut milk

2 ounces chopped dark chocolate
  (about ½ cup)

½ cup water

½ teaspoon ground cinnamon

⅛ teaspoon cayenne or chili powder
  (optional)

1 teaspoon vanilla extract

4 small fresh bananas

⅓ cup chopped hazelnuts

⅓ cup pitted and halved cherries

Place the frozen bananas and coconut milk in the container of a food processor or a high-powered blender like a Vitamix, and blend until smooth and creamy. Don't overprocess or you risk melting the bananas. Serve immediately in the banana splits or place the banana ice cream in the freezer, and when ready to serve let the ice cream sit at room temperature for a few minutes to soften slightly.

Place chocolate in a medium bowl. Bring water to a boil in an electric kettle, and pour ½ cup into the bowl with the chocolate. Let sit 10 minutes without stirring. Carefully drain as much water as possible from the bowl and immediately stir in the cinnamon, cayenne or chili powder, and vanilla until the mixture is smooth. Stir in additional hot water, 1 tablespoon at a time, if needed to reach a smoother consistency.

Split the fresh bananas down the middle lengthwise and place on serving plates. Top each with scoops of banana ice cream, chocolate sauce, hazelnuts, and cherries.

Blueberry Dessert Soup

A medley of carefully matched ingredients makes this dessert soup a terrific way to cap off a steamy summer day. It also makes a fetching appetizer for a dinner party, shower, or backyard gathering with good friends.　　*Serves 6*　　*V, G, L*

3 cups wild blueberries or 4 cups larger cultivated ones, plus more for garnish

¾ cup plain, 2% Greek yogurt, plus more for garnish

½ cup unsweetened almond milk

Juice of ½ lemon

2 tablespoons chopped fresh mint or ½ teaspoon peppermint extract

2 tablespoons honey or pure maple syrup

1 teaspoon minced fresh ginger (optional)

½ teaspoon ground allspice

Chopped pecans or unsalted raw or roasted almonds, for garnish (optional)

Place the blueberries, yogurt, almond milk, lemon juice, mint, sweetener, ginger if using, and allspice in a blender or food processor container, and blend until smooth.

Strain the mixture through a fine-mesh sieve into a bowl to remove any remaining skins. Refrigerate the soup for at least 2 hours before serving. If the mixture becomes too thick upon chilling, simply stir in some additional milk.

To serve, ladle the soup into serving bowls and garnish with whole blueberries, a dollop of Greek yogurt, and chopped nuts if desired.

Top: BLUEBERRY DESSERT SOUP, *page 111*

Bottom: CHERRY GRANITA, *page 113*

Cherry Granita

Granita is Sicily's rustic take on sorbet and an ideal low-calorie treat to keep your cool. The key to achieving snowflake-like perfection is not to let the mixture freeze into a solid block, so watch the clock. This recipe is also great with pomegranate or blueberry juice.   *Serves 6   V, G, L*

2 cups cherry juice

½ cup granulated sugar of choice

1 teaspoon grated orange zest

½ teaspoon almond extract

¼ teaspoon ground cloves

Pinch of sea salt

Fresh mint or whole cherries, for garnish (optional)

Place the cherry juice, sugar, orange zest, almond extract, cloves, and salt in a blender container, and blend until well combined. Pour the mixture into a large, shallow, freezerproof container. Cover with a lid or aluminum foil and transfer to the freezer.

Freeze until ice crystals start forming around the edges and the mixture looks mushy, about 2 ½ hours. Do not let the mixture freeze solid. With the tines of a fork, scrape the ice crystals into the center of the container and return to the freezer. Scrape the ice crystals about every 45 minutes afterward until all the liquid has frozen into small crystals, roughly five times.

When ready to serve, spoon the granita into serving bowls, and garnish with fresh mint or a whole cherry if desired. Leftovers will keep in the freezer for about 1 month, if kept covered in an airtight container.

PB&J Pops

Here's a frosty spin on the iconic sandwich that both adults and young ones will enjoy. If desired, use raspberries in lieu of strawberries.

Serves 4   V, G, L

2 cups chopped strawberries

2 tablespoons honey or agave syrup

⅔ cup evaporated milk

⅓ cup plus 1 tablespoon natural unsalted peanut butter

1 teaspoon vanilla extract

Add the strawberries and honey to a food processor or blender container, and blend until smooth. Pour the strawberry puree into a fine-mesh sieve set over a bowl and press down with a spatula or wooden spoon. Discard the seeds and reserve the puree.

In a medium bowl, whisk the milk into the peanut butter 2 tablespoons at a time, until silky smooth.

Spoon half of the peanut butter mixture into four standard-size Popsicle molds. Top each with an equal amount of the strawberry puree and finish with the remaining peanut butter. You should have two layers of peanut butter and a single layer of strawberry. Freeze until solid, about 4 hours. If you're having trouble unmolding the Popsicles, run the molds under warm (not hot) water to loosen.

Raspberry Mint Frozen Yogurt

Most store-bought frozen yogurt is loaded with processed sugars, artificial flavorings, and other questionable ingredients. Thankfully, homemade fro-yo whipped up without an ice cream maker is far from a high-flying kitchen feat. Simply blend together tangy Greek yogurt with any sweet seasonal fruit, such as raspberries, cherries, or strawberries, and stir at regular intervals. If you don't mind a few extra calories, it's best to make this with 2% Greek yogurt. Nonfat won't produce the same nice creamy texture.　　*Serves 6　　G, V, L*

2 cups raspberries

2 cups plain 2% Greek yogurt, divided

3 tablespoons honey

1 teaspoon vanilla extract or almond extract

¼ cup finely chopped fresh mint

Juice of ½ lemon

1 teaspoon grated lemon zest

Chopped almonds, for topping (optional)

Grated dark chocolate, for topping (optional)

Place the raspberries in a blender or food processor container and blend until smooth. Pour the raspberry puree into a fine-mesh sieve set over a bowl and press down with a spatula or wooden spoon to separate the seeds. (Skip this step if using seedless fruit such as blueberries or pitted cherries.) Discard the seeds and return the raspberry puree to the blender or food processor container along with 1 cup yogurt, honey, flavor extract, mint, lemon juice, and lemon zest. Blend until smooth.

Pour the mixture into a shallow container, fold in the remaining 1 cup yogurt, cover tightly, and freeze for about 45 minutes. Remove the container from the freezer, take off the cover, and, using a spatula, stir in the icy bits from the edges and mix with the softer center until smooth. Return to the freezer for another 30 minutes and stir again. Repeat this process every 30 minutes for 3 hours. Make sure to stir until smooth each time before returning the container to the freezer to prevent too many ice crystals from forming. It's a good idea to set a timer so you don't forget to stir the mixture.

When ready to serve, take out the desired amount of frozen yogurt from the freezer and let sit at room temperature for several minutes to soften. Serve topped with almonds and grated chocolate if desired. Extras can be kept in the freezer for up to 2 weeks.

Top: RASPBERRY MINT FROZEN YOGURT, *page 115*

Bottom: AVOCADO CHOCOLATE MOUSSE, *page 117*

Avocado Chocolate Mousse

Avocado lends this no-fuss chocolate mousse a rich, creamy texture that will have you coming back for more. The secret is not to use avocados that are too hard or too soft, either of which will impart an overly strong avocado flavor. You could even try the same recipe using pumpkin puree or soft tofu. Garnish options include cocao nibs, shaved dark chocolate, raspberries, or coconut flakes.   *Serves 6   V, G*

2 large avocados, flesh scooped out

1 large ripe banana

⅓ cup unsweetened cocoa powder

¼ cup coconut milk

¼ cup pure maple syrup

1 teaspoon grated orange zest

1 teaspoon vanilla extract or chocolate extract

½ teaspoon ground cinnamon

⅛ teaspoon chili powder or cayenne powder (optional)

Pinch of sea salt

Place all the ingredients in a food processor or blender container and blend until smooth, scraping down the sides as needed. Serve immediately or the mousse can be placed in an airtight container in the refrigerator for up to 2 days.

To serve, place the mixture in serving bowls and garnish as desired.

Chai Chia Pudding

Chia seeds are a nutritional gold mine and a natural thickener that helps create a tapioca pudding–like texture. They are increasingly available in health food stores, well-stocked bulk shops, and some larger supermarkets. The chai-infused water adds an interesting flavor nuance, while the dates contribute natural sweetness. To punch things up, garnish with one or more of the following items: chopped dried or fresh apricots, pistachios or other nuts, flaked coconut, fresh berries, a drizzle of maple syrup.   *Serves 6   V, G, L*

1 cup raw unsalted cashews

4 cups water

4 chai tea bags

1 cup pitted dates

2 tablespoons pure maple syrup (optional)

1½ teaspoons vanilla extract

½ cup chia seeds

Place the cashews in a bowl, cover with water, and soak for at least 2 hours.

Bring the 4 cups water to a boil in an electric kettle, and pour into a large heatproof bowl along with the chai tea bags. Let steep 10 minutes. Remove the tea bags, add the dates to the bowl, and let cool to room temperature.

Drain the cashews and place them in a blender or food processor container along with the chai and date mixture, maple syrup if using, and vanilla. Blend until very smooth.

Pour the blended mixture into a large bowl along with the chia seeds and whisk well. Let stand for 15 minutes, whisking every few minutes to prevent clumping. Cover the bowl and refrigerate for at least 3 hours before serving.

Very Berry Trifle

Light and airy angel food cake soaks up the juices of berries wonderfully in this no-fuss version of trifle, a traditional British dessert involving layers of cake and fruit anointed with whipped cream. You can make it more grown up by including some port in the berry mixture. Also, feel free to swap out any of these berries for others such as blackberries, strawberries, or boysenberries. It's best to chill your beaters and bowl before making whipped cream. *Serves 6* *V*

1 cup raspberries, plus more for garnish

1 cup blueberries, plus more for garnish

1 cup fresh currants, plus more for garnish

2 tablespoons poppy seeds

2 tablespoons honey or pure maple syrup

1 store-bought angel food cake

1 cup cold whipping cream

¼ teaspoon grated nutmeg

1 teaspoon vanilla extract

Place the berries, poppy seeds, and sweetener in a food processor or blender container, and pulse several times until well combined but not to the point of making berry juice.

Slice the angel food cake into 2-inch cubes and place them in a large bowl. Pour the berry mixture over the cake, cover, and refrigerate for at least 4 hours.

In a deep bowl, beat the whipping cream with an electric mixer or a whisk until soft peaks form. Beat in the nutmeg and vanilla.

Spoon the fruit-soaked cake into serving bowls, and top with whipped cream and whole berries.

Top: VERY BERRY TRIFLE, *page 119*

Bottom: COCONUT CREAM PIE MILKSHAKE, *page 121*

Coconut Cream Pie Milkshake

If you love coconut cream pie, here's a way to re-create its flavor without firing up the oven. The result is the perfect sultry-night dessert drink to sip. You can find slabs of frozen coconut in Asian markets or alongside frozen fruits in many supermarkets. I like a stronger coconut flavor and richer shake, so often I use a mixture of coconut milk and cow's milk as my liquid base. Try whole milk for an indulgent shake.   *Serves 2   V, G*

1½ cups milk of choice

1 cup chopped frozen coconut meat

1 large banana, preferably frozen

2 heaping tablespoons graham crumbs, plus more for garnish

¼ cup macadamia nuts

1 tablespoon honey

¼ teaspoon grated nutmeg, plus more for garnish

1 teaspoon vanilla extract

Place all the ingredients in a blender or food processor container and blend until smooth, about 1 minute. Running your machine for at least 1 minute will help break down the coconut for a smoother consistency.

Pour into serving glasses and garnish with additional graham crumbs or freshly grated nutmeg.

Matcha White Chocolate Bites

I'm definitely a dark chocolate kind of guy, but if matcha could speak it would say to white chocolate: "You complete me." Matcha is a verdant green tea powder bursting with antioxidants, while the blended cashews give these cups a creamy texture. If you're not using silicone molds, you may want to use paper liners for easier unmolding. Or a quick dip of the tray bottom in warm water can help get these treats out.   *Serves 12*   *V, G, L*

½ cup whole unsalted raw cashews

2 cups water, divided

7 ounces chopped white chocolate (about 2 cups)

2 teaspoons matcha powder

1½ teaspoons vanilla extract

1 teaspoon ground ginger (optional)

Place the cashews in a bowl, cover with water, and soak for at least 2 hours.

Bring 1 cup water to a boil in an electric kettle, and add boiled water along with the white chocolate to a medium heatproof bowl. Let sit for 10 minutes.

Meanwhile, drain the cashews and place in a blender container along with the matcha, vanilla, ginger if using, and another 1 cup cold water. Blend until very smooth.

Carefully drain off as much liquid as possible from the white chocolate and stir until smooth. Pour in the cashew mixture and stir to combine.

Divide the mixture among 12 mini muffin cups or ice cube molds. Place in the freezer until set, about 4 hours. Unmold the matcha cups and store in an airtight container or zip-top bag in the freezer until ready to serve.

No-Bake Flourless Fig Brownies

Think of these as brownies with a fudgy personality. Warning: They are habit forming. And they actually get better after a day or two in the refrigerator. For a bit of kick, consider adding a touch of cayenne or chili powder. You could use pitted dates rather than figs as your base, but they won't be as rich tasting. Even try rolling the mixture into balls for brownie bites. Don't send the fig-soaking liquid down the drain. Instead, use it in smoothies or when making oatmeal.   *Serves 12   V, G, L*

1½ cups dried Mission figs, stems removed

1 cup almond flour

½ cup unsweetened cocoa powder

¼ cup unsalted almond butter or other nut butter of choice

3 tablespoons pure maple syrup

1 teaspoon vanilla extract or chocolate extract

1 teaspoon instant espresso powder (optional)

1 teaspoon ground cinnamon

⅛ teaspoon sea salt

½ cup chopped walnuts

Place the figs in a bowl, cover with water, and soak for 2 hours.

Drain the figs and place them in a food processor container along with the almond flour, cocoa powder, almond butter, maple syrup, flavor extract, espresso powder if using, cinnamon, and salt. Blend until the mixture begins to clump together. Pulse in the walnuts.

Place the mixture in a greased or parchment paper–lined 8-inch-square pan. Using damp fingers, press the mixture into the pan until about ¾ inch thick. Place in the refrigerator to firm up, about 1 hour. Slice into 12 squares to serve.

Top: NO-BAKE FLOURLESS FIG BROWNIES, *page 123*

Bottom: INDIVIDUAL FRUIT CRISPS WITH VANILLA-SCENTED YOGURT, *page 125*

Individual Fruit Crisps with Vanilla-Scented Yogurt

When berries and peaches are at their sun-kissed best, there's no reason to cook the heck out of them in the oven. The crisp topping includes gluten-free quinoa flakes, which are made by passing the grains through a roller to flatten them. You can also substitute rolled oats or spelt flakes for equally good results.   *Serves 6   V, G*

3 cups mixed berries of choice, such as blueberries, raspberries, and blackberries

2 ripe peaches, chopped

4 tablespoons pure maple syrup, divided

2 tablespoons cacao nibs (optional)

1 cup pecans

½ cup walnuts

⅓ cup quinoa flakes

2 tablespoons ground flaxseed

½ teaspoon ground cinnamon

¼ teaspoon ground cardamom

Pinch of sea salt

1 cup plain, low-fat Greek yogurt

1 teaspoon vanilla extract

In a large bowl, toss together the berries, peaches, 2 tablespoons maple syrup, and cocoa nibs if using. Place the pecans, walnuts, quinoa flakes, flaxseed, cinnamon, cardamom, salt, and remaining 2 tablespoons maple syrup in a food processor container, and blend until the mixture is just slightly chunky. In a bowl, stir together the yogurt and vanilla.

To serve, divide the fruit mixture among serving bowls and top with the nut mixture and vanilla yogurt. Be sure to mix the components just before serving.

Lemon Cheesecake with Cherry Sauce

You can serve up a truly decadent-tasting cheesecake without giving the oven a workout. The addition of oats, raisins, walnuts, and cherries ensures this delectable dessert has a lot of nutritional merit. And turning out this cake will be a snap if you use a springform pan, which features sides that can be removed from the base. If needed, use oats labeled "gluten-free." *Serves 8* *V, L*

Cheesecake:

1½ cups rolled oats

½ cup walnuts

1 cup raisins

¼ cup neutral-tasting oil like grapeseed or canola

1-inch piece fresh ginger, grated or very finely minced or 1 teaspoon ground ginger

8 ounces cream cheese, room temperature

⅔ cup reduced-fat ricotta cheese

½ cup confectioners' (powdered) sugar

Grated zest and juice of 1 lemon

Cherry Sauce:

1 cup pitted cherries

2 tablespoons honey, agave syrup, or granulated sugar

1 teaspoon vanilla extract

⅛ teaspoon ground cloves

For the cheesecake: Place the oats and walnuts in a food processor container and process until pulverized. Add the raisins, oil, and ginger. Process until the mixture begins to stick together and everything is moist.

Line a 9-inch springform pan or regular cake pan with parchment paper cut to fit the bottom. Pour the oat mixture into the prepared pan and press down firmly to form an even crust. Refrigerate while you make the filling.

In a large bowl, mix together the cream cheese, ricotta cheese, sugar, lemon zest, and lemon juice until smooth. Pour the cheese mixture over the oat crust and spread out flat with a spatula. Refrigerate the cheesecake for several hours.

For the cherry sauce: Combine the cherries, sweetener, vanilla, and cloves in a food processor or blender container, and blend until smooth. Strain the cherry mixture through a fine-mesh sieve into a bowl, stirring and pressing with a wooden spoon or spatula to remove any skins. Discard the skins and reserve the cherry sauce.

Serve slices of cheesecake topped with cherry sauce.

Top: LEMON CHEESECAKE WITH CHERRY SAUCE, *page 126*
Bottom: PINEAPPLE CARPACCIO WITH POMEGRANATE AND GINGER WATER, *page 128*

Pineapple Carpaccio with Pomegranate and Ginger Water

Traditionally, carpaccio involves razor-thin slices of raw beef, but the same concept can spill over into dessert. And there's no better contender than pineapple. A whisper of salt heightens the flavor of the fruit. Each of the components can be prepared a few days in advance and then assembled as needed. To remove the seeds (arils) from a pomegranate without turning your kitchen into a scene from *Dexter*, slice the fruit into quarters and submerge in a bowl of cold water. Pull apart the pomegranate so that the seeds sink to the bottom and the white membranes float to the top. Remove the membranes and drain to recover the seeds.   *Serves 6*   *V, G*

½ cup water

1 tablespoon chopped fresh ginger

2 tablespoons honey or agave syrup

1 ripe pineapple

⅛ teaspoon sea salt

Seeds of 1 pomegranate (about 1 cup)

Grated zest of 1 lime

2 tablespoons finely chopped fresh mint

Bring water to a boil in an electric kettle. Add ½ cup boiled water along with the ginger to a heatproof bowl, and let cool to room temperature. Place the ginger and water in a blender container along with the sweetener, and blend for 1 minute. Strain the mixture through a fine-mesh sieve into a bowl to remove any remaining solids. Discard the solids and reserve the ginger-flavored water.

Slice the top and bottom off the pineapple. Stand the pineapple upright and slice off the skin, following the curve of the fruit. Cut the peeled pineapple in half lengthwise and then slice the two pieces of fruit crosswise as thinly as possible.

Spread the slices, slightly overlapping, on serving plates and top with a very light sprinkle of salt. Drizzle ginger water over the top and garnish with pomegranate seeds, lime zest, and mint.

Mango Fool

A deliciously simple British dessert, a fool — the word hails from the French *foule*, meaning pressed or crushed — is traditionally made by folding sweetened fruit into cream. Thick Greek yogurt is a healthy substitute for cream, but it's best to use one with a little bit of fat still left in for a richer-tasting dessert. The mixture will keep in the refrigerator for about five days.   *Serves 6   V, G, L*

2 large ripe mangoes

1 teaspoon grated orange zest

Juice of ½ orange

1 teaspoon grated or finely minced fresh ginger

1½ cups plain, 2% Greek yogurt

2 tablespoons honey or agave syrup

1 teaspoon vanilla extract or ½ teaspoon almond extract

Dash of ground cloves (optional)

¼ cup chopped macadamia nuts or slivered almonds, for garnish

Fresh mint, for garnish (optional)

For the garnish, peel about 12 ribbons from the flesh of 1 mango using a vegetable peeler and set aside. Cube the remaining flesh from the mangoes. If desired, set aside some small cubes for the garnish instead of peeling ribbons.

Place the mango cubes as well as the orange zest, orange juice, and ginger in a food processor or blender container and blend until smooth. If needed, add a small amount of water to help with the blending.

In a large bowl, stir together the yogurt, sweetener, flavor extract, and cloves if using. Gently fold the mixture into the mango puree. Refrigerate for at least 1 hour before serving.

Serve in dessert bowls or glasses garnished with mango ribbons or cubes, nuts, and fresh mint if using.

Top: MANGO FOOL, *page 129*

Bottom: ALMOND THUMBPRINT COOKIES, *page 131*

Almond Thumbprint Cookies

These oven-free cookies are so rich, you'll be surprised how satisfied you are with just one. Rather than use store-bought flour, you could place whole nuts and rolled oats in a food processor and grind them into a texture similar to flour. Be sure to look for jam or preserves that contain more fruit than sugar. If you need to make the cookies free of gluten, you can use oat flour labeled "gluten-free."   *Serves 16   V, L*

1 cup almond or hazelnut flour

1 cup oat flour

¾ cup unsalted almond butter or other nut butter

⅓ cup pure maple syrup or honey

½ teaspoon almond extract

½ teaspoon ground cinnamon

¼ teaspoon ground cardamom

⅛ teaspoon sea salt

⅓ cup raspberry or strawberry jam or preserves

Place the flours, almond butter, maple syrup or honey, almond extract, cinnamon, cardamom, and salt in a food processor container, and blend until the mixture begins to clump together. If it looks too dry, add some more nut butter or liquid sweetener.

Roll the dough into 1-inch balls, flatten slightly, and make an indentation with your thumb in the center of each (almost as if making mini bowls). If the sides of the cookie begin to split, simply mold them back together. Fill each cookie with jam. Refrigerate the cookies for about 2 hours before serving.

Vanilla Ice Cream Cupcakes

Like trail mix, these whimsical treats are full of goodies. The fruit and nut cups, vanilla-infused creamy filling and luscious chocolate sauce team up to create a dessert that will bring the chef many kind words. To liquefy hardened coconut oil, simply place the amount needed in a small bowl set in a larger bowl of hot water. Don't let any water mix with the oil, however. Let sit for a couple minutes and then stir. The cups should not be assembled until just before serving, but the unfilled pecan cups and the cashew ice cream can be kept covered in the freezer for a couple of weeks. Keep the chocolate sauce in the refrigerator for up to a week.   *Serves 12   V, L*

Ice Cream:

1 cup unsalted raw cashews

½ cup plus 2 tablespoons cold water

1 vanilla bean

2 large frozen bananas, chopped

3 teaspoons vanilla extract

Crust:

1 cup pitted dates

1½ cups pecans

½ cup wheat germ

¼ cup pure maple syrup, honey, or agave syrup

⅛ teaspoon sea salt

Chocolate Sauce:

½ cup coconut milk

⅓ cup liquefied coconut oil

¼ cup unsweetened cocoa powder

3 tablespoons pure maple syrup or agave syrup

½ teaspoon ground cinnamon

2 teaspoons chocolate extract (optional)

⅛ teaspoon cayenne (optional)

Coconut flakes, for garnish (optional)

For the ice cream: Place the cashews in a bowl, cover with water, and soak for about 2 hours. Drain the cashews and place them in a blender or food processor container along with the ½ cup plus 2 tablespoons cold water. Blend until smooth. With a sharp knife, slice down the length of the vanilla bean and scrape the seeds into the cashew cream. Add the frozen banana and vanilla extract, and blend until smooth. Place the mixture in the freezer for about 4 hours. You will likely need to let the ice cream sit at room temperature for several minutes to soften before serving.

For the crust: Place the dates in a bowl, cover with water, and soak for about 30 minutes. Place the pecans in the bowl of a food processor and grind into small bits. Add the soaked drained dates, wheat germ, sweetener, and salt. Process until the mixture sticks together when pinched between your fingers.

Divide the crust dough into 12 equal balls and place each in a standard-sized greased muffin cup. Press the crust down and up the sides of the muffin cups to form a bowl. Place the muffin tray in the freezer for about 1 hour.

For the chocolate sauce: Place the coconut milk, coconut oil, cocoa powder, sweetener, cinnamon, and chocolate extract and cayenne if using in a blender or food processor container, and blend until smooth. Add more coconut milk if needed to reach the desired consistency.

Run a knife around the edges of the pecan cups to remove them from the pan. To serve, add a dollop of ice cream to a pecan cup and top with chocolate sauce and coconut flakes if using.

Fruity Dessert Pizzas

Who says pizza has to be savory or even baked in the oven? These sweet individual dessert pizzas bejeweled with colorful fruit and pistachios are sure to be a hit with everyone in your family. Silken firm or silken extra-firm tofu such as the brand Morinaga are soft forms of tofu that can be found packaged in aseptic boxes in supermarkets. They can be used to make wonderful sweet spreads without tasting beany. Don't confuse it with regular firm tofu, which is much too hard for this purpose. In lieu of tofu, trusty cream cheese works here, too. You can find sandwich thins in most supermarket bread aisles. Another great garnish option is to combine 2 tablespoons granulated sugar with 2 teaspoons cinnamon and sprinkle over the top.   *Serves 8   V, L*

12 ounces (1 box) silken firm or extra-firm tofu, drained or 8 ounces cream cheese, room temperature

½ cup confectioners' (powdered) sugar

2 teaspoons vanilla extract

1 teaspoon grated orange zest

8 whole wheat sandwich thins, separated into halves

3 cups mixed fruits, such as blueberries, raspberries, strawberries, peach slices, chopped kiwifruit, and chopped banana

⅓ cup chopped pistachios

2 tablespoons honey

Place the tofu or cream cheese, sugar, vanilla extract, and orange zest in a blender or food processor container, and blend until smooth.

Toast the sandwich thin halves until browned and crisp. Spread the tofu or cream cheese mixture over the toasted bread halves and top with the fruit and pistachios. Drizzle honey over the top.

Top: FRUITY DESSERT PIZZAS, *page 134*

Bottom: COFFEE ICE CREAM FLOAT, *page 136*

Coffee Ice Cream Float

This dessert is a pretty simple affair, but it's far from an ordinary soda float. Though I give instructions for combining everything in a blender, my preferred method for making the float is to steep the coffee, cocoa, and cardamom together in a coffee press such as a Bodum so that the cocoa and cardamom have a better chance of dissolving into the brewed coffee. You would then stir in the vanilla once everything has steeped together. You can serve the coffee hot or cooled based on your preference. Cinnamon or nutmeg can stand in for the cardamom if you prefer.   *Serves 2   V, G*

2 cups brewed coffee

2 tablespoons cocoa powder

⅛ teaspoon ground cardamom

1 teaspoon vanilla extract

½ teaspoon ground cinnamon

2 generous scoops vanilla, chocolate, or mocha ice cream

2 tablespoons chopped almonds or hazelnuts (optional)

Place the coffee, cocoa powder, cardamom, and vanilla extract in a blender container and blend until smooth.

Pour into desired glasses or mugs, add ice cream, and top with nuts if using.

Carrot Cake Muffins

These oven-free individual carrot cakes are a little moister than the baked version, but no less palate pleasing. You can also bake the batter in a standard square baking pan and then slice into squares. If you want the topping to remain really white for presentation purposes, you can swap out the maple syrup for white sugar.   *Serves 10   V, G, L*

1 cup chopped pitted dates

2 cups shredded carrot

2 cups almond flour

⅓ cup unsweetened dried coconut

1 teaspoon ground cinnamon

1 teaspoon ground ginger

¼ teaspoon ground cardamom

Pinch of sea salt

⅓ cup cream cheese, reduced-fat if desired

1 tablespoon pure maple syrup

1 teaspoon vanilla extract

Grated orange zest, for garnish

Place the chopped dates in a bowl, cover with water, and soak for 1 hour, or until softened. Place the soaked, drained dates in a food processor container and blend to a pastelike consistency.

Place the shredded carrot in a colander and squeeze out as much liquid as possible, or press in a clean kitchen towel. Add the carrot, almond flour, coconut, cinnamon, ginger, cardamom, and salt to the food processor container with the dates, and blend until the mixture sticks together.

Divide the mixture among 10 standard-sized lightly greased or parchment paper–lined muffin cups and press down to pack in the contents. Place the tray in the freezer until the muffins are set, about 1 hour.

Meanwhile, stir together the cream cheese, maple syrup, and vanilla. Unmold the muffins and spread an equal amount of the cream cheese mixture on the top of each. Top each with a small sprinkle of orange zest. Refrigerate until ready to serve.

Top: CARROT CAKE MUFFINS, *page 137*

Bottom: APPLESAUCE PIE, *page 139*

Applesauce Pie

Can't master the art of making pie crust? Not to worry, as this dessert possesses many of the same cherished flavors of apple pie or apple crisp without the need to roll out a pie crust. I prefer not to peel the apples since that's where the majority of fiber and antioxidants are found.   *Serves 8   V, L*

Filling:

4 large red-skinned apples, chopped

3 tablespoons graham crumbs

2 tablespoons granulated sugar of choice

Grated zest of 1 lemon

1 teaspoon vanilla extract

¾ teaspoon ground cinnamon

½ teaspoon ground ginger

¼ teaspoon ground cloves

¼ teaspoon grated nutmeg

Pinch of sea salt

Crust:

¾ cup unsalted raw or toasted almonds or other nuts like walnuts or pecans

2 cups rolled or quick-cook oats

¼ cup hemp seeds (optional)

1 cup dried cranberries or dried cherries

⅓ cup neutral-tasting oil such as canola or grapeseed

¼ cup honey

½ teaspoon ground cinnamon

Vanilla ice cream or frozen yogurt (optional)

For the filling: Place the apples, graham crumbs, sugar, lemon zest, vanilla extract, ¾ teaspoon cinnamon, ginger, cloves, nutmeg, and salt in a food processor container and blend until the mixture is slightly chunky. Do not blend until completely smooth. Remove the apple mixture from the container and set aside.

For the crust: Place the nuts in the cleaned food processor container, and process until broken down into small pieces. Add the oats, hemp seeds if using, cranberries or cherries, oil, honey, and ½ teaspoon cinnamon to the container. Process until everything is moist and the mixture sticks together when pinched between your fingers. Add more honey if the mixture seems too crumbly.

Lightly grease an 8-inch cake or tart pan. Pour the nut mixture into the pan and press firmly so the bottom and sides are covered. Place the pan in the freezer for 30 minutes to set.

Pour the apple mixture onto the crust and spread it evenly. Refrigerate the pie for about 1 hour before serving. Serve slices topped with vanilla ice cream or frozen yogurt, if desired.

Watermelon Slushies

Ideal for the dog days of summer, this refreshing slush is a cinch to make. A brain freeze never tasted so good. Refrigerate and simply blend with some more ice when ready to serve.   *Serves 2   V, G*

8 ice cubes

2 cups cubed watermelon

½ cup orange juice

2 tablespoons chopped fresh mint or basil

1 tablespoon honey or agave syrup

Combine all the ingredients in a blender or food processor container, and process until you have a "slushie" consistency. Don't overblend into a completely smooth texture. Best served in a glass with a small spoon.

Product Resources

Bear Naked

www.bearnaked.com

A selection of praiseworthy granola options.

Bob's Red Mill

www.bobsredmill.com

My go-to source for no-cook essentials like oats, milk powder, and almond flour.

California Olive Ranch

www.californiaoliveranch.com

Gourmet-tasting extra virgin olive oil without the painful price tag.

Eden Foods

www.edenfoods.com

A good source for organic canned items such as beans packed in BPA-free cans.

La Tortilla Factory

www.latortillafactory.com

A stellar range of tortillas worthy of rolling up even the fanciest of ingredients.

Manitoba Harvest

www.manitobaharvest.com

A forward-thinking company providing an array of hemp foods such hemp hearts (seeds) and hemp milk.

MatchaSource

www.matchasource.com

A great place to score top-notch matcha green tea powder. A splurge never tasted so good.

Navitas Naturals

www.navitasnaturals.com

A wide range of no-cook superfoods like cocoa powder, acai powder, and goldenberries.

Nielsen-Massey

www.nielsenmassey.com

An excellent source for vanilla, almond, lemon, and other flavor extracts.

Nutiva

www.nutiva.com

A one-stop shop for all things coconut, hemp, and chia. Slathering their coconut butter on a piece of toast is near utopia.

Raincoast Trading

www.raincoasttrading.com

Some of the best canned salmon, tuna, and sardines around, packaged in BPA-free tins. I'm particularly fond of their no-salt-added canned salmon.

Sun-Maid

www.sunmaid.com

Plenty of dried fruit options that are of consistently good quality.

Thai Kitchen

www.thaikitchen.com

Rice noodles, fish sauce, and coconut milk for infusing your no-cook recipes with Asian flair.

Wild Planet

www.wildplanetfoods.com

A selection of gourmet-tasting and sustainably caught canned seafood. Like Raincoast Trading, they also use BPA-free tins.

Zico

www.zico.com

Ultra-refreshing coconut water for blending into your next smoothie.

Conversions

Measure	Equivalent	Metric
1 teaspoon	---	5 milliliters
1 tablespoon	3 teaspoons	14.8 milliliters
1 cup	16 tablespoons	236.8 milliliters
1 pint	2 cups	473.6 milliliters
1 quart	4 cups	947.2 milliliters
1 liter	4 cups + 3½ tablespoons	1000 milliliters
1 ounce (dry)	2 tablespoons	28.35 grams
1 pound	16 ounces	453.49 grams
2.21 pounds	35.3 ounces	1 kilogram

Index

V

W

Z

Acknowledgments

No cookbook is a one-person show. Thank you to the hard-working farmers at the St. Jacob's Farmer's Market near my hometown of Waterloo, Ontario, for providing city folk with real food. I continue to be appreciative of Kelly Reed at Ulysses Press for her hard work in making my cookbooks the best they can be. Of all the magazine editors I work with, those at *Alive* magazine allow me the most freedom in the kitchen, which has greatly improved my culinary skills. Joan and John Macarthur, your never-ending support is never forgotten. There are worse gigs, but a big high five to Robert Waldeck for having the willing palate to try out many of the recipes that populate this book. Though we no longer see each other as much we should, Mom, Dad, and brother Glen, I can't express enough how much my professional success over the years has been tied to your support. Most importantly, I can't thank enough my loving partner and recipe guinea pig, Tabi Ferguson. Without you, I would be nowhere near the cook or man that I am today.

About the Author

Matt Kadey is a registered dietitian, freelance nutrition writer, recipe developer, and travel photographer based in Waterloo, Ontario, Canada. A prolific magazine writer, his nutrition, recipe, and travel articles have appeared in dozens of prestigious publications including *Men's Health, Alive, Women's Health, Shape, Prevention, Eating Well, Canadian Living, Men's Journal, Vegetarian Times, Runner's World, Bicycling,* and *Fit Pregnancy.* He is also the author of *Muffin Tin Chef: 101 Savory Snacks, Adorable Appetizers, Enticing Entrees & Delicious Desserts.* An avid cyclist, Matt has cycled and feasted his way through numerous countries including New Zealand, Myanmar, Sri Lanka, Laos, Thailand, Cuba, Ireland, Ethiopia, Belize, and Jordan. He is also a former provincial mountain bike champion in his age category. You can find Matt at mattkadey.com and muffintinmania.com.